# FIND YOUR FIT

*Three Steps to Choosing a Best-Fit College Major and Career*

## DUSTIN PETERSON

DUSTIN PETERSON
www.dustinpeterson.org

Printed Worldwide
First Printing 2023
First Edition 2023

ISBN: 979-8393335502

Cover Design by Bryan Peterson at Peterson Ray & Company

# FIND YOUR FIT

To Samye, without whom the story of this book wouldn't exist.

# Table of Contents

# Acknowledgements

Like any great career, a book only comes to fruition through the efforts of a community. In this case the community included people who inspired me, shared their story, or traversed my own career journey right along with me, experiencing the ups and downs along the way.

I've been blessed with a best friend and eternal companion who has lived the highs and lows from the front seat, and we're both better for it. Thank you to Samye for trusting the process, including returning the chocolate chips to save three dollars, volunteering to earn enough credits for free clothes and supplies, and being unashamed to repurpose a chair or table on the curb to save a buck and support my career path, which didn't always yield a great ROI.

Emily and Cade are both an inspiration to me for their willingness to be vulnerable and embrace uncertainty, then do the hard work of reflection to figure out the next step. They figured it out and are an example to others of how to do what they love with courage and confidence!

Lindsey is a gifted editor who sees the potential in a project and makes it more than it could have been. She took what I thought was a nearly finished product, unwound it, and wound it back up into a tighter, more cohesive, and relatable project that not only guides the reader but hits to the heart. Thank you, Lindsey!

I'm grateful for the many clients over the years who have trusted my advice, shared their story, and embraced risk, being different, and doing what they love. This book is the accumulation of lessons learned and insights gleaned from thousands of conversations over more than 15 years.

Most importantly, thank *you* for reading the book. I exist to help people maximize their potential and do what they love, but that only happens if you trust me enough to give the process here a try. Your motivation and desire to contribute to the greater good is inspiring. We, the world, need you!

# This Is the Perfect Book for You if...

You need help choosing your college major and career.

Do you dread the question, "So, what are you going to do with your life?" or any of its variations, e.g. "What's next?" or "What are you going to major in?" or "What will you do when you graduate?" When people ask you any of these questions, do you give them a canned answer? Or say something you think they want to hear just to make them go away?

Do you sometimes feel like everyone except you has life figured out? You talk with your friends or family members, and they all seem to have a plan, making you wonder if you missed a step somewhere along the line or skipped the class where people made life plans?

Are you drawn to all sorts of different majors and career paths and can't seem to narrow it down to just one? Do you like lots of different activities and have different hobbies that you can't imagine fitting into any one career path?

Does the thought of spending your whole career in one field make you apprehensive? Do you look at people older than you who have been in their career for a tremendous amount of time and wonder how on earth they stayed the course for so long?

Are you being asked by your college or a career counselor to "pick a path" and declare a major, and you keep procrastinating the decision because you can't make up your mind? More importantly, do you feel anxious and stressed about even having to decide?

Do you feel stuck? You know there's something out there for you, but you don't even know where to begin to look to figure out what it is. Do you sometimes say to yourself, "If I could just figure out my path, I would give my whole heart and soul to it, but I don't even know where to start..."?

If any of these statements resonates with you, this book is definitely for you. Like you, I've said each of these statements — out loud or in my mind — multiple times over the course of my career and often felt like the answer was just out of reach.

*Find Your Fit* is for you. By the end of this book, you'll have not only clear answers to these questions, but also a solid plan for what to do next.

# Chapter 1

## This is the Sweet Spot

When I was teaching leadership at Rice University, I ran this rogue career coaching operation in my office. I say "rogue" because I wasn't working in the career office; I was with the Office of Civic Engagement teaching leadership courses. But, because of my own struggle in college and the fact that I had found my way, I helped a few students here and there and word got out fast.

Almost daily, students would walk into my office, shut the door, and whisper, "Hey, I hear you can help me figure out my life." I'm not entirely sure why they would whisper, except that not knowing what to do with your life can feel like a vulnerable and lonely place to be.

They would start to tell me what they were majoring in and how much they hated it, then we'd get onto the business of figuring out a new path. Most often when they would share their declared major with me, I'd ask them a critical question that you should answer now: **Why *that* major? Tell me about <u>the moment</u> when you decided *that major* was for you.**

Almost never — at least that I can remember now — have I had someone say, "You know, I'll never forget when I discovered this deep-seated passion for X that is totally aligned with my talents and interests and what I do best."

About 99% of the time, they would pause, think long and hard, searching for the moment, then say something like, "I'm not sure. I guess it was when my teacher said…" or "My parents just told me…" or "I watched a show and…" or "It's only X number of credit hours…" or "It pays really well…" or [insert your favorite extrinsic motivator}.

I heard the same pattern repeated again and again.

These students felt completely lost. They felt discouraged. They could sense a seed of inspiration that they had something important to do, but couldn't seem to pinpoint it. They came to me feeling anxious, stressed, and overwhelmed by the messages they'd been socialized into for the past 17-25 years. They were searching for answers and as a consequence, were willing to listen to just about anyone who might help them.

The problem was that they had no strategy for sorting through the myriad voices. Not only were they stressed and overwhelmed, they were often paralyzed when it came to decision making because there were too many options and the pressure to make exactly the right choice felt immense.

Does that sound familiar to you at all? That is why I wrote this book. I can help.

I want everyone who reads this book to take a breath, lower the stakes, trust themselves, and realize that career is a journey, not a single event. I want you to be intentional in your decision-making and stop looking everywhere but internally for answers about what to do with your life. You've got what you need inside you right now to make a well-educated decision about your major. I can help you home in on the relevant information and then strategize what to do with it.

Figuring out what to do with your life does feel like a weighty decision. For whatever reason, "What am I going to do with my life" — what I call the "universal question — is the one question we all struggle with, but few have found the answer to. Why is that? And why is it so difficult to figure out? If we are meant to live lives of purpose and meaning, then why do so many of us trudge along doing meaningless things?

I've learned over decades of helping people answer that question that the prime time to figure it out is *today*. As in, now. Don't wait. As the adage goes: the best time to plant a tree was 20 years ago. The second-best time is now.

I've also learned that if I had received some guidance from ages 18–25 — even just some basic mentoring — I could have saved myself years of confusion, frustration, and misdirection in choosing a college major and career. You can begin to get clarity in your teen years, but often lack enough experience to truly figure it out. You can also figure it out in your late 20's, 30's, 40's and beyond, but you are more susceptible to external forces keeping you stuck, like a mortgage, student loan debt, growing family, community or religious roles and obligations, and more.

Looking back, I believe the sweet spot for answering the universal question is your college and graduate school years; you are more mentally mature than you were in high school, a bit more responsible, less tethered to things, often with less familial obligations, and more open to exploration, creativity, and pursuit of passion. You are used to living below your means, flexible to move almost anywhere geographically, and hungry to figure out your purpose. It's no wonder that most people look back on their time in college wistfully. It's a time of discovery!

Discovery is the goal of this book — to help you find greater clarity and confidence than ever before about the answer to the big questions you're asking yourself in college. I want to first take you through my personal journey in hopes that it might be illustrative to you. I remember when I was struggling to answer that question and I would read as many bios, personal histories, and narratives as I could about how people got to where they are. I usually felt like their stories fell short, like they left out the best part: the struggle, the fight, the revelation, and ultimately the victory. Most people have a bio that reads like, "I studied X, took a job at Y company, and am now the President of Z." The reality is, the space in between X, Y, and Z is fraught with dissonance, fear, anxiety, confusion, risk, and ultimately reward. I want you to see the ups and downs of the career journey. I promise to tell the whole truth, and nothing but it.

I also want to profile several people who have achieved great clarity and are on the path toward doing something they love. Reading the stories of others can be inspiring but they can also give you insights into how to pursue your own journey.

Most importantly, I want to pull back the curtain on the method I've used for more than 15 years as a career coach at dustinpeterson.org to help people at every stage of life to discover their best-fit college major, career, and beyond. Discovering your passion and purpose isn't strictly formulaic, but there is certainly a system you can follow to gain clarity and move forward with confidence and conviction. I want to walk you through that process.

By the end of this quick read, you'll have narrowed down a short list of best-fit college majors or career paths that could yield great satisfaction, productivity, and meaning. The price you'll have to pay to get there is some intensively honest self-reflection, research, exploration, and connecting with those who can help you on your journey.

The good news is that the chapters in this book are short and the content is engaging. I only write books I would have the patience to read. That said, if you don't *engage* with the activities, you'll walk away clearer about the process but no clearer about *your path*. So, get a pen and paper and get ready to pay the price! Let's dive in and figure out which majors fit for you.

# Chapter 2

## The Universal Question

"What should I do with my life?"

I've never met a single person who didn't wrestle with this question or some variation of it. I certainly have, and if you're reading this book, you probably have too.

The first time I can recall being asked what I would do with my life was at a youth conference when I was 15. I gathered with at least a thousand other young people from northeast Texas on the campus of Austin College in Sherman, Texas (famous for its mayonnaise factory and the scent that would permeate the campus when a stiff wind hit). We spent the week in classes, teambuilding, dances, meals, a talent show, and other activities meant to strengthen our faith and build our confidence.

On the first day, I was put with a group of 30 peers, and we kicked off with a quick icebreaker: introduce yourself by sharing your name, where you're from, and what you hoped to do for a living one day. I was somewhere in the middle of the pack, thankfully. As the first few youth began the introductions they seemed to have confident answers to that last question. "I'm Sarah from Dallas, and I'm going to be a doctor," or "I'm Chris from Plano, and I'm joining the army." What the heck? How did they know this? And why had I never thought about my future career until that moment?

My anxiety started to rise as the introductions headed my way. Before I knew it, it was my turn.

"I'm Dustin, and I'm from Dallas…" I said. And then in an almost revelatory way, I blurted, "…And I'm going to be the President of the United States." A few people laughed, a few whistled, and everyone cheered. I felt a total rush. Wow. That felt good.

I'll skip to the end here for a moment: I'm not the President of the U.S. Frankly, I believe that would be a terrible job. However, I don't think what I really was after was the presidency. I think that was the first moment when my inner voice spoke out and framed an internal desire in a simplistic way that I didn't have the language to communicate as a 15-year-old. I labeled something that was actually much more dynamic.

What I really wanted was to inspire, influence, lead, motivate, teach, guide, speak, and create change. And at that time, in my naive and undeveloped brain, that was what I perceived the president did. Regardless, it did the trick and the introductions moved on, but I didn't. I sat with that thought and pondered how it felt. Throughout the week, people would jokingly greet me as Mr. President, and I liked the way it sounded — teenage ego at its best. But it also held a clue about what I wanted to do with my life.

The same is true for you. Whenever I help a young person figure out their college major, I always take them through a 60-minute interview. I'll walk you through it later step-by-step, but I'll tell you now how it always starts: take me back to your childhood or youth — as far back as you remember — what did you think you might do with your life?

What's funny is that people either have no idea or they get embarrassed and say, "Oh I don't know...a _____ maybe?" or "Well, it was kind of dumb and I laugh to think about it now, but _____." But the answer isn't what matters. The key is what the answer reveals about what's really in their core.

More on this later. For now, let's pause and consider the scope of the work we're doing in this book.

When I meet with students about choosing a major, they've often got rigid ideas about what that decision means. They think there is one right choice and everything else is wrong. They believe that college major implies a limited set of career prospects which in turn imply a specific overall quality of life. This is not an accurate depiction of reality. The reality is that there are likely several majors that could be the right choice for you.

The other problem with this line of thinking is that it puts undue pressure on the decision of college major. I promised you the truth and here it is: your major can affect your job prospects, but it alone doesn't determine your career or future happiness. Choosing a major is an important decision, but it doesn't lock you into a single track. It is also not the last decision you'll make about what to do with your life. Rather it is part of a career-long process.

That said, if you can get clear about where you might want to be in the future, you harness the power of being intentional, as in living life on purpose. It turns out those early experiences in life can carry important clues about where you might fit in the bigger scheme of things. Our goal in this book is to look for themes that have already emerged in your life and use that information to connect you to a major and career options that tap your unique talents and give you fulfillment.

Before we continue, let me repeat. You're just making the decision that is in front of you right now. There are probably several options that fit for you. In this book, we will work through a process that can help you make an intentional decision about your college major. You can also use this same process in the future as you come to other career decisions that arise along your path.

Alas, I did not have this guidance, so I left that youth conference and forgot about it altogether, assuming I would figure it out when the time came to go to college and declare a major.

Suffice to say, when the time came to start at Ricks College in Rexburg, Idaho, and to declare a major, they didn't have a major for President of the United States, so I took a first stab at...psychology. I know. Not political science, Mr. President? I looked through the classes in the course catalog and political science seemed really boring, and I figured psychology would help me understand (read: manipulate) people, which seemed like what politicians and the President do — remember, teenage brain. Plus, I had taken a psychology class in high school that was semi-interesting. So, there you go. I'd be a psychology major. It didn't last long.

I walked into my first psychology class and sat down at the back of an auditorium-style room to listen to a lecture about something psychological. I went home that day, read Chapter One, prepared for a quiz (which I bombed) and said, "Forget this. Too intellectual," and then promptly changed my major. The irony is that I now spend my days having intellectual conversations with leaders on psychology-based concepts like motivation, influence, and building relationships. But at the time, I didn't even give it a chance. On to the next one!

And so began the roulette wheel of majors. Spin the wheel and hope something sticks. I tried English, Business, Organizational Behavior, Sociology, Marketing, Seminary, and ultimately Public Relations. With each major, I'd declare it, dabble in it, bail after a class or two — mostly based on gut feeling — and try something else. What I was doing — that I didn't realize I was doing — is the same thing that you are doing, have done in the past, or will do in the near future if you're not careful. I was succumbing to the outside/in model of college major choice.

# Chapter 3

## The Outside/In Model

Think for a moment about how you've approached choosing a college major until now. What factors are influencing your decision-making process?

You might be surprised to learn that there's a fair amount of research about how people choose a college major. According to research, the top factors influencing college major choice — in order of importance — are below:

1. Parents — 19%!
2. Teachers
3. Siblings
4. Friends
5. Media
6. Future earnings
7. Future opportunities

(Malgwi, et al., 2005; DeMarie & Young, 2003; Pearson & Dellman, 1997; Lowe & Simons, 1997)

Let's consider a few of these:

- Parents: The #1 influencer. Almost 20% of first-year college students choose their major based on parental influence, as in, "No, you won't go to that college that costs all that money and major in *that!*" Or, "I'm a dentist, your grandfather was a dentist, and your great-grandfather was a dentist. Son, you're going to be a dentist." (As if career runs in the bloodline…. Lawyering or accounting is a gene that gets passed down?)

- Teachers: I can think of at least a dozen students I've coached over the years who chose their college major because they had a teacher in high school they liked. I'll ask how in the world they decided to be a math major, and they'll remark, "Oh, I really liked my high school math teacher my sophomore year, Mr. Marsh. He was so nice and told me I was good at math. I want to be just like him!" Again, as if the goal of four years of expensive college and a 40-year career is to mimic the teacher you liked for a year when you were 15.

- Siblings: This one is pretty self-explanatory. "My brother is a salesman, so I think I'll do it too." See the note above about genes and hereditary majors. They don't exist.

- Friends: Worse than siblings, this influencer is rooted in the pack mentality. "My buddy is going to be an engineer, and he and I are close, so I think I'll do it too because we're inseparable." True, until you each get different jobs at graduation — him in Alaska, you in Kansas, and suddenly you become separable.

- Media: This one is interesting in the way it manifests. I've coached many a student who has watched a medical or legal drama and come away saying, "I just want to save lives like that!" or "I want to fight for what's right, just like those lawyers!" only to graduate with loads of student loan debt and no option but to take a soul-sucking corporate job or high-paying medical specialty that deprives them of joy, but pays the bills. Meanwhile, the job is nothing like what they saw on tv. The media can portray careers in the least realistic of lights, and we are suckers for idealism.

- Future earnings and opportunities: I'll lump these together and state the obvious — people often choose a major because "I just want to make great money" or "the outlook for IT specialists looks good." Look, neither of these is a wholly wrong way to look at your career, but they also aren't the *best* way to look at your career, as I'll show you later in the book.

Of course, there are many other factors that didn't make the list. Things like:

- Prestige
- Power
- Position
- Title
- Geographic location
- Number of credit hours needed to graduate
- And more!

What do you notice about these influencing factors?

They all come from the outside. They're what are called *extrinsic factors*, meaning factors outside of yourself.

There's no shortage of these external pressures. The question is, so what? So what if you pick your major based on money? Parental influence? Geographic location (I just want to live in Hawaii!)?

Apparently, lots of people do it that way. In fact, I'd venture to say that this is the way your parents chose their path, and probably their parents did as well. So, what's the big deal?

The better question is, what's the *cost*?

I often ask this question in seminars after walking through the data, and a thousand hands shoot up, mostly those of older people who have been in their careers for a decade or so. They are quick to share the cost because they've experienced it (or are experiencing it in the present). In fact, anyone who has made a major life choice based on an extrinsic factor knows the price you pay.

The first thing audiences say is happiness. When you choose something for money, to please others, or for another extrinsic reason, you risk giving up happiness. You find yourself doing something every day that holds no meaning or joy for you. Soon you are going through the motions and your satisfaction declines. Given that roughly one-third of human life is dedicated to work, you can see how that might be a problem.

I typically press whoever offers this answer first to take it a step or two further. "Then what?" I'll ask. They'll say that people who are less satisfied and happy are less productive at work, which is true. And when people are less happy and productive, they get promoted less, make less money, quit more often, bring their work home, self-medicate to escape from their jobs, and ultimately don't last.

True, true, and true some more.

Research from Benabou and Tirole (2003) in *The Review of Economic Studies* shows that the shelf life on extrinsic factors is always short and finite. What's a shelf life? Put simply, it's the amount of time a ham and mayonnaise sandwich will last on the counter before it goes bad. Like, two hours. Think of any of the aforementioned factors like a ham and mayo sandwich. They'll satisfy in the short-term — maybe even motivate you — but will ultimately disappoint. And, once they cease to motivate, they may even act as a demotivator, negatively impacting your future motivation to undertake a similar task and/or undermining future performance but sapping your energy and drive.

You may say, "But I only want to make $100k a year." And guess what? That will motivate you...until the day you make $100k a year. At which point, believe it or not, it will cease to satisfy. You'll subconsciously raise the bar on yourself and now you need $150k to be at peace.

Or you might say, "I just want to be a lawyer like my mom." That will drive you, believe me. For all those years of school you'll be motivated...until the day you walk across the stage at graduation. The second you have that diploma and get your first job and find yourself sitting at the desk of your new firm staring out the window as you draft yet another contract to make a salary and pay off your debt, it will cease to satisfy. Why? Because you didn't do it for you. You did it to satiate an extrinsic factor.

By the way, this is no indictment on lawyers or doctors or any other profession. It's not about the profession, but rather the way you choose.

I call it the outside/in model. It looks like this:

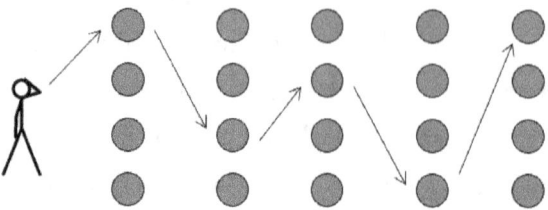

In this model, you have a choice to make. Let's start with "choosing a college major." In the absence of clarity about how to make this decision, you look OUT at your options, which are typically limited to just a few — pick one arbitrarily based on an extrinsic factor — then cram yourself IN to that major. What happens next? You discover that it's not what you thought it was. "Huh. This isn't anything like that medical drama. Microbiology is the worst." The trouble is, you lack a defined way to make your next choice, so you default to the same method. Look OUT there, pick something else, and cram yourself IN to that option. Over and over again.

The outside/in model will always leave you empty. It never works in the long-term.

**The outside/in model at work**

A few years back I was interviewing a young lady for an ecclesiastical endorsement to get into Brigham Young University (the Utah one). We sat down and I started the interview by asking her to tell me her story. She shared about her upbringing, her interests and passions, and her long-term goals. It was all very inspiring. I then asked, "So why BYU? What was it about that place that drew you in?" She paused thoughtfully and then said in this peaceful way, "It's the trees."

I stumbled. "The...trees, you say?"

"Yes," she said. "We did a campus visit, and I was so impressed by all the trees. It's so green and beautiful. And I thought to myself, I want to be around all these trees."

Not the coursework. Or the college major choice. The trees.

"Huh. Are you going to study trees? Be an arborist, perhaps?"

"Oh...no." She chuckled. "English."

The outside/in model in full effect.

Now, to be fair, she probably found her way and probably even had a tremendous experience above and beyond the trees. And kudos to BYU's grounds department. You sold at least one student on a major life choice based solely on the beauty of your work. Impressive!

But I guarantee that the trees ceased to be a driving factor the day she showed up to freshman statistics and got her syllabus. Or after the first snowfall when those trees turned white, and the temperature became insufferable.

She's not alone. I obviously was a sucker for this model.

**How I chose my major**

Remember, I had seven majors in five years of college. Eek. I'm the guy who signed up for an astronomy class my freshman year because I figured it would tee me up to take girls on dates and impress them with my understanding of the constellations as we sat on a blanket staring at the stars. No kidding. Turns out astronomy is *physics* in disguise. What!? Who knew. I certainly didn't, which resulted in one of two Ds I got in college. (The second? Dating and Marriage Prep. I figured it would be loaded with girls to meet, which was true. It was about a 40:3 ratio, except no one cared about an 18-year-old freshman so I never went to class, turned in no assignments, and failed.)

**With each successive major, I opted in for an extrinsic reason and opted out for the same reason.** In fact, after testing out classes from six different majors, the university notified me that I had too many credit hours without officially declaring a major and that I needed to choose something or I'd be asked to leave (in much more diplomatic language than that). The heat was on. It was time to commit.

So, I decided to do the rational thing and schedule a visit with the Career Center to get some insight from a trained professional about the major I should choose. I showed up at the scheduled time and met with a guy — we'll call him "Gus" — for my appointment. I was pumped. I wasn't exactly sure what to expect, but I assumed this guy would do some Jedi mind-reading and reveal to me my destiny. Reality was a bit farther from the truth.

I sat down with Gus for a conversation, and, after a bit of chit chat, he asked me a great question. "So, what do you like to do? What are you good at?"

Good start. I stared out the window, a bit puzzled that I was struggling so much to come up with something, then shared, "Well, I like working with people."

Gus brightened a bit. "So, you like working with…the public?" He seemed like he was onto something, like a hound on a scent.

"Yes! Definitely."

"Would you say you can relate well with the public?" Gus asked.

Hmmm. "Yes...?" I said.

He sat back, pleased. "You should try public relations."

The Jedi master had spoken.

I asked him about public relations. As in, what is that? He shared that these professionals are called on to connect with the public, share information about clients, build relationships, etc. I thought, "Huh...never heard of it. Sounds like it could be a perfect fit." And just like that, after one 30-minute discussion, I had found my fit.

Note the overreliance on a career advisor as a total manifestation of the outside/in model. Could have just as well been a parent, teacher, mentor, family member, or Google. In reality, no one — not even me — can tell you what to choose. No one knows you like you know you. Even a trained professional really can't have a clue in 30 minutes. In fact, the people who know you well would probably be better career advisors in some ways than someone who has known you for half an hour. The whole world of career advising is, to me, a flawed industry, because it is often built on short, superficial conversations that assume that the client has a certain level of self-awareness that most of us simply don't have. Alas, I'll save that ax to grind on a different book.

I left with energy because of the clarity I felt. I was going to go all in on my newfound major with gusto and pride, signing up for all required courses and diving in headlong. I remember feeling totally committed to becoming the very best public relations practitioner in the program. Imagine my surprise when several classes into the major I was bored. Or perhaps not so much *bored* as disengaged and left wondering, "What did Gus see in me that made him think this was the right fit?"

It was not a fit. In fact, to me it was downright dull. I would sit through classes and complete projects and look for the spark of interest, but it wasn't there. This isn't intended to take anything away from the great teachers, by the way. This was a byproduct of a bad *fit*.

But, like any good student, I soldiered on, figuring that perhaps it would get better when I graduated. Sneak peek: it didn't. And sidenote: if you ever find yourself saying, "It will probably get better when…" for more than six months, it won't get better.

Regardless, I graduated in public relations and began my search for my first post-graduation gig. I hustled and found a job at a premium PR firm based in Dallas, gave it my all, and discovered within a few short months that the work was just as misaligned with who I am as I suspected. In fact, I only lasted nine months and bolted for something new. For more on that story, check out my book *RESET: How to Get Paid and Love What You Do*. I'll spare the gruesome details here; suffice to say, the outside/in model did what it does best — took my tuition money, zapped my energy, and left me feeling empty.

If you're headed down this same path, feeling disengaged and tired, know that you're not alone. Unfortunately, most of us do career the same way.

A few years back, I met Ana at a workshop for college counselors. She sat in the front row, just to the left of me, and seemed super engaged. She was especially energetic when I shared my story of the career counselor I had in college who told me I should go into public relations because "I relate well with people…the public…" in spite of the fact that I wanted to be a teacher.

After the workshop, she came up to me excitedly and said, "You told my story!"

When she was in college, she took a psychology class and loved it, so she registered as a psychology major. But shortly after, she met with a career counselor who said, "You won't make any money in that" and recommended she switch to…English? As if that would make her more money, right?

She persisted as an English major despite not enjoying it and got a job as an English teacher after college. She didn't enjoy it at all but did it for seven years. Seven years! Right around the time when she was thinking about switching jobs, a mentor said they were looking for an English teacher at the collegiate level, but she needed a Master's, and they offered to pay for her schooling. The next thing she knew, she was getting a degree in the very thing she didn't like, only to graduate and teach it in college.

Then she woke up one day and said, "I can't do this anymore."

A career search and a few connections led her to a job as a career counselor at a major university, where she uses her aptitude for…psychology…to help people pursue a vocation instead of just a job.

Here's a woman who was fascinated by psychology but felt internal dissonance because of an extrinsic push by an advisor, only to eventually circle back to the very thing she felt drawn to in the first place. Now she's thriving and getting paid to do what she loves. She's satisfied, successful, and growing each day.

In our analogy, she chose a ham and mayo sandwich and left it on the counter way too long before she realized it would never sustain her. It left her feeling empty. It wasn't until she abandoned the outside/in model that she found her way to a more fulfilling career.

I've just given you three examples of the outside/in model leaving people empty. I could share hundreds of these stories because I've worked with so many people who approached their major and career decisions this way. I'm thinking of my client who chose to be a dentist because his parents were both dentists. He showed up at our first coaching session looking and feeling drained and devoid of energy. Or my client who chose oil and gas to make a good salary but felt like it was total drudgery…but also couldn't afford to leave and do something else because the pay was too good. Or the client who got an MBA, believing it would create clarity and open doors, only to call me after completing it to say, "So…what now? I'm no clearer."

There *has* to be a better way. Right? If the outside/in model will always leave us disappointed in the long run, is there a better way to make major life decisions?

There is. Can you guess what it's called?

# Chapter 4

## The Inside/Out Model

You guessed it. In fact, in workshops and seminars I ask this same question, "Any guess what the better way is called?" Inevitably, someone raises their hand and says proudly, "The inside/out model!"

To which I say, "Yes! So, what is that model? How does it work?" Usually, they become less confident and start to hesitate, even though they know in their gut what the model is all about. You likely do as well.

They'll eventually say, "I guess it probably means that you take some time to find out about who you are and use that to decide if something is a fit...?"

Nailed it.

**The inside/out model says that the best way to make important decisions — college major, specialty, career, and beyond — is to first get radically clear about who you are at your best, then use that information as a lens to screen out options and find the best-fit choice that most aligns with who you are.**

The inside/out model looks something like this:

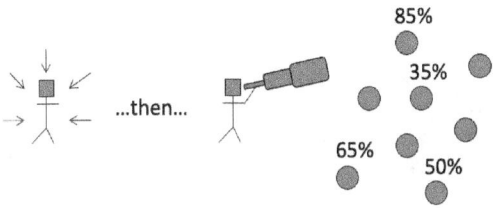

Notice that the arrows around the individual are pointing inward, meaning that he or she is spending all the energy previously directed at extrinsic efforts now at internal ones, getting crystal clear about self. They are then using that information as a lens of sorts, looking out at the options in the world to determine the one that appears to be most aligned based on information about themself. Where one option seems to be a 35% fit and another an 85% fit, they are choosing the latter, giving themselves the greatest chance of success based on one key word: fit.

Let me say that again. The inside/out model is all about finding options that fit (and there will likely be more than one), meaning they are aligned with who you are as an individual.

The next logical question is, what would you need to know about yourself to make a clear-headed decision about your next step? There are lots of things, but a few might be:

- Passions
- Purpose
- Values
- Strengths
- Personality Type
- Motivations
- Aspirations
- Vision
- Skills
- Aptitudes
- Tendencies
- Weaknesses

- Blind spots
- Goals
- And more!

The list could go on because you are truly a complex and dynamic individual. You can't be sorted into a major by a career assessment or an online quiz, and certainly not by a 30-minute conversation with an advisor. You are made of strengths and weaknesses, triggers and motivators, values and beliefs, blind spots and shadow sides, vulnerabilities and preferences, and a whole life story that has shaped your character to be who you are today. Developing a sense of clarity about who you are is a lifelong process, and the clearer you get, the more adept you'll become at making decisions that align with who you are.

That's the goal in this book. I'll guide you through the process to getting clear about yourself in the coming chapters, but before I do, I want to share what happens when people approach their college major and career decisions this way. It takes effort, but the reward is great.

**Benefits of inside/out decision-making**

So, let's say that you get radically clear about yourself, and you use that information to find a best-fit major that aligns with the best of who you are. What would you expect to be the outcome? In other words, if someone chooses a college major and eventually a job based on alignment to self, what would you expect to see as a result?

I've found that three things happen when people make inside/out career choices:

- More satisfaction and energy. In a research study from Shamir and Eilam in *Leadership Quarterly,* the researchers found that those who live and lead congruent to their authentic selves experience five key outcomes:

    1.  Greater resilience, meaning the ability to bounce back from challenge, difficulty, and failure.
    2.  Higher job satisfaction, meaning more joy and fulfillment in work.
    3.  Increased productivity.
    4.  More "flow," which is a term used to describe the state of getting lost in your work, feeling passionate and motivated, losing track of time, and feeling powerful.
    5.  They develop authentic followers, meaning that they motivate those around them to be their best, authentic selves, and they give others permission to bring their whole selves to the work they do.

- Higher success rate. If satisfaction and energy go up, what would you expect to be the next naturally occurring outcome? Success increases. When we do what we're good at, we do it well and become more successful. It's a virtuous cycle. The more we do work that aligns with what we do best, the better we become at that work, the more success we experience, and the more motivated we feel to do more of it!

- Potentially more money depending on market demand for your skills. I'll discuss this one in depth toward the end of the book, but for now I'll suggest this: what happens when someone does what they're good at, experiences satisfaction and energy, and becomes more successful at it? What would you guess is the result in the workplace? You're right — the money comes. That's how business works. Those who do what they're good at and are successful are also more productive and, as a result, we pay them more money to keep doing what they do best. Notice the caveat of "depending on market demand for your skills." That's not meant to be a cop out. Frankly, I believe in almost any field you'll get paid more for doing what you love than those who do it just to earn a paycheck. But there are certainly industries where you won't make as much as quickly as you'd like. Regardless, the formula still holds true: do what you do best, increase satisfaction, boost success, make more money.

People who make aligned decisions experience dramatically different results. That's because things like passions, purpose, values, strengths, motivators, and so on are called intrinsic motivations, and unlike extrinsic motivations, intrinsic ones have the shelf life of a Twinkie — forever. The burn rate on making internally aligned decisions is long, stable, and motivating.

Let me give you some examples.

### Emily's Story

Emily is just now getting started in her college major. I first met Emily when she came by our house for a dinner appointment as a missionary for the Church of Jesus Christ of Latter-Day Saints. As I do when we're getting to know any other missionary, I asked about her story. She talked about her family, her upbringing in Utah, and her year of school at Utah State prior to serving a mission. I asked about her plan for after her 18-month mission was complete. She said she'd probably go to dental school to be a hygienist. I asked more but could sense that she wasn't totally resolved. I resisted the urge to climb onto my oversized soap box and preach about inside/out and instead gave her a copy of my book, *TALENTED: Discovering and Using Your God-Given Talents to Find More Joy in Life.* She went on with her mission and was an amazing missionary.

After she returned home, we kept in touch with her via Facebook until I got the following text one day:

I just wanted to reach out and say thanks for everything you've done for me. You counseled me to use my talents to pursue a career where I could serve, heal, and help people thrive and obtain a better quality of life. Not gonna lie, this kinda threw me for a loop because for years I had planned on going into dental hygiene.

During my mission I would have thoughts that I should consider changing my major, but I always pushed them aside because I didn't want to change my plan. When I got home from my mission I did a lot of praying, studying and I read your book TALENTED, and the answer came so clearly that I should go into physical therapy. So, before the semester started, I switched my major to kinesiology and exercise science, and I'm now on track to study physical therapy, and it has been one of the best decisions I've ever made! I have never felt more at peace with my education, and I'm genuinely so excited about where I am headed. I finally feel a connection between God's will and my education, which hasn't happened for me before.

I just finished my first week at my new job as a physical therapist aide, and it has been such an amazing and rewarding week! You talked a lot in your book about finding where you get your energy from, and holy cow, this is it for me! I have already loved every minute of it, and I truly feel like this is God's path for me right now.

Inside/out is the way.

Emily is aligned with and connected to the path that she's chosen. She's already found a job in the field. She's hungry to learn and she's experiencing high satisfaction. This is the goal. You can do this too. You have what you need right now to get started. Note that she doesn't have all of her career moves mapped out for the next decade. She has simply used what she knows about herself to get into a learning and working situation where she can use her talents on the regular and derive energy, growth, and fulfillment from the experiences she's having.

Trent is further along on his journey, but his approach was the same.

**Trent's Story**

Trent is a good soul. From the moment he came into my office at Rice University I felt a deep connection with him. At 18 years old, he was exceptionally reflective, self-aware, and internally motivated. He was initially on a pre-medicine track because of some volunteer programs in high school, but he felt unsettled.

We talked several times and he was an early adopter of the inside/out model. In fact, it drove every decision he made in college, from classes he chose to activities he opted into. The thing about Trent is that he felt this dissonance between doing something that made sense logically and working in a traditional job (becoming a physician), and following his heart and contributing in a way that would likely make no money, but that would yield tremendous satisfaction (becoming a cognitive scientist, serving with a non-profit, and/or taking his love of meditation and yoga to the world).

As a high school student, he was a self-proclaimed science nerd. In fact, he was on the middle school Science Olympiad team. Because of his draw to science and supportive parents, he interned at labs throughout high school, at one point doing nano-particle research focused on cancer solving particles.

But as much as he loved the science, what ultimately drove him was a desire to enhance human life. He didn't want to be disconnected from the human element. He wanted to serve patients, not just be a researcher in the lab.

He began applying to top-notch bio-engineering programs and getting accepted (think: Stanford), but had an important moment in November of his senior year. He was staying with his dad's Iranian teacher friend on a trip and having a conversation about the future. This wise friend bottom-lined Trent at one point and asked point blank, "so do you want to be a physician or an engineer?"

Trent said, "I think a bio-engineer."

"Do you realize what classes you're going to take as an engineer? Physics, thermodynamics, calculus...," the friend said.

Trent asked, "Wait, but when do I get to take the exciting classes in English? History?"

"There'll be no time for that!" the friend said. Those who have majored in engineering are likely nodding their heads. It's "all in."

Trent thought about this, and ultimately concluded that he cared about the human side and bioengineering wouldn't help him with this.

His dad's friend gave him a short list of colleges with programs that hybridized his interests — science that benefits people but with human interaction. He chose Rice because, in his words, the climate was better than Brown and started down a pre-med route because medicine was one of the ultimate ways to contribute to human well-being.

Interestingly, Trent also was in a time of spiritual exploration. He had been reading about spirituality and eastern philosophies and felt in his gut that Rice would provide a better environment for him to pursue this interest in tandem with his love for science. He was right. He had a chance to go to Nepal after his freshman year, learned yoga, and brought Sadhguru, a world-renowned yogi, to campus for a talk. Trent took religion classes, meditated often, and became a more spiritual person, noting that the high-school-Trent wouldn't recognize the college-Trent.

I asked him many years later what moment led to his ultimate transition out of pre-med and into cognitive science, the degree he ultimately graduated with. He said, "It wasn't a moment as much as a process." He noted that he came to Rice to be a physician but even his peers would often say, "Trent, you're not going to be a physician." It just wasn't what was in his heart. As he said to me, "Making a difference can happen in far more exciting and compelling ways."

Ultimately, Trent graduated in cognitive science and pursued a more data science angle through additional education. This background and his interests led him to an artificial intelligence engineering company, followed by a job at a health and wellness technology firm, and now with a non-profit focused on raising human consciousness around nature and our connection to it, and particularly with saving the soil for future generations — an initiative founded and supported by Sadhguru, the yogi and mystic Trent brought to campus many years earlier.

During the pandemic, I had a chance to catch up with Trent via Zoom. He was living in a rural community in Tennessee enjoying a life of stillness at the Isha Institute of Inner-Sciences in Tennessee. He had spent the pandemic traveling around India, practicing yoga, increasing his consciousness, and practicing what he preaches: contributing to human well-being.

What gives Trent's story so much power is his connection with his values and his willingness to explore options with openness and curiosity. On the surface, the connections between pre-med, artificial intelligence, soil conservation, and yoga may not be obvious. But for Trent as a unique individual, they make complete sense. They tell a story of exploration and progressive learning about one-self with an eye toward improving life for other humans.

You have a unique story to live too.

Making decisions from the inside/out along your career journey is a sure-fire way to stay aligned, authentic, and congruent with your values. Like Emily and Trent — whether you are just starting out or deep into your journey — putting who you are in the center of your process will ultimately yield satisfaction.

**Prioritize fit first**

Before we end this section, let me be crystal clear about an important point. I'm simply saying that the best way to make career decisions is to prioritize fit *first*. I'm not suggesting that you exclude all other factors from your decision-making process.

This disclaimer is mostly for the parents reading this book and saying, "Rubbish! This guy isn't realistic at all. If you follow his advice, you'll end up as a florist." Which, by the way, is a great job. More on that later in the money section. But the important point is this: are extrinsic motivators a *bad thing?* Like, is it wrong and evil to pursue a major or career that makes you boatloads of money? Or is it *bad* to pursue something that your parents or friends think you'd be good at? Or are you doing the wrong thing to be an accountant like every other member of your family?

The short answer is a resounding NO.

However, and it's a big however, **extrinsic motivators should never be in the first position when making a decision.** They can be in positions two through ten, but never number one. What does that mean?

Well, when making a decision, the only thing you should consider *first* is fit. Ask yourself, *does this fit with who I am?* If the answer is "yes," then I don't really care what other factors you consider as you make your decision. Number two could be money, as in, does it make me lots of money? If so, great. Or it could be parents, as in, will it please my parents? Great. Or it could be geographic location, as in, can I live in Hawaii while doing it? If so, super. But when you are making a list of the factors that are contributing to your decision, the first position should always be fit.

GOOD:

1. **<u>FIT</u>**
2. Money
3. Location
4. Parents
5. Just like the TV show
6. Good future career opportunities

BAD:

1. Money
2. **<u>FIT</u>**
3. Location
4. Parents
5. Just like the TV show
6. Good future career opportunities

Why shouldn't you put anything else in position number one? Easy. We looked at this in the previous chapter. Extrinsic factors have a short shelf-life and will ultimately leave you feeling empty. If you choose a major or career for money, you'll get exactly what you seek: money. And what you may not get is a good fit. Remember the ham sandwich analogy. You'll wake up one day in the future making great money in a job you hate. Or if you choose because of your parents, you'll get exactly what you seek: approval from your parents…and potentially a job you hate. You'll get to sit at a fancy desk doing a job that's misaligned, but your parents will be thrilled to ask you all about it each time you visit. Or if you choose a job for geographic location, you'll get to live in the mountains or on the beach but spend your nine-to-five grinding away at a bad-fit job. If you're reading this book, I'm guessing you want to avoid that misery. Skip the ham sandwiches and choose the Twinkie.

Choose fit first; anything else can follow.

# Chapter 5

## What Holds You Back?

This seems like a good point to stop and consider an important question: If the inside/out model is where it's at, and the outcomes are so great, then why don't we all do it?

I'll tell you what I've observed in my work with clients. There are a handful of factors in play here. The first set of factors have to do with lacking a clear understanding of yourself and the second group of factors have to do with fear. Let's look at each of those.

**Unclear understanding of the self**

Why don't we already know ourselves? If we carry around all this uniqueness throughout our lives, why do we seem to be so unclear about who we are?

There are a few reasons.

1. Self-knowledge gets buried

First, the self-knowledge gets buried. Think of yourself like an onion. I sometimes tell audiences that the time when you were your most authentic self was when you were in kindergarten. You didn't know any better! You showed up in spaces with friends and were just yourself, saying and doing things that were natural and authentic to you. Perhaps you didn't have the words to articulate your uniqueness, but you certainly weren't yet afraid to be yourself.

But very quickly, society began to bear down on you. As you showed interests, aptitudes, passions, talents, or other aspects of your identity, the world around you would give you messages about what aspects of you were "okay" and which ones weren't. "You can't do that" or "you're not good enough" or "that's not acceptable."

Over time, you built up layers of the onion as protection against your vulnerabilities being exposed. And soon enough, the only things you really manifested or even knew about yourself were those superficial things that others could see — your personality, personal appearance, and maybe a few interests. Now, your authentic self is trapped beneath the layers.

2. Mona Lisa Syndrome

The second reason we don't know ourselves is what I call "Mona Lisa Syndrome." What makes the Mona Lisa so interesting? I have no idea, but I'm also not an art aficionado.

However, lots of other people do know what makes her so interesting, and they travel across the globe to see her.

She's amazing.

Here's the thing: she doesn't know she's amazing.

She sits in her frame looking out at the people walking by and wonders, Why do these people stop and stare? What do they see? Is there something behind me? What's so interesting?

She doesn't get it. She doesn't know how awesome she is because of this important principle:

It's hard to see the picture when you're in the frame.

Likewise, you might have little to no idea what makes you unique, but other people do. If I gathered 20 of your closest friends, family, and colleagues into a room and asked them what makes you great, they'd probably identify five to ten consistent things that make you uniquely you.

But you can't see it.

Herein lies the great paradox of self: the only person who doesn't seem to know what you do best is you. Why? Because who you are is so natural, innate, and fluid. Your talents, and values, and passions are so much a part of who you are that you don't work to deploy them. They express naturally in your life and work.

Imagine figuring out who you are, then using that information to guide the way you work. What if you could identify what you do best and use that as the foundation for your career and leadership? Better yet, don't imagine, go do it.

How?

The same way Mona Lisa would finally see her beauty — have someone hold up a mirror and tell her.

Start by asking the people who would fly across the globe to see you what they see. When have they seen you at your best? What did they see? And why did it have an impact on them?

Uncomfortable? Sure. But not more uncomfortable than not knowing.

And the answer, applied to your work, just may change your whole trajectory.

3. It's tough to filter out the noise

Throughout your career journey, you'll likely have many people chip in advice, words of wisdom, and personal anecdotes. Some will be empowering, others challenging, and some will be just plain dumb. A key attribute of those who succeed in finding a career they love is learning which voices to tune out and which to amplify.

So how do you decide?

It's not as easy as simply listening to the ones who make you feel good and tuning out the ones who make you feel bad. It's all about who is giving you the advice.

<u>Parents/Close Family Members/Spouse/Significant Other</u>

If your parent, close family member, spouse or significant other is giving you advice, sharing insights, or relating concerns, you should listen. Even if their fears seem crazy and unfounded, your relationship with them is more important than a career. You owe it to them to listen and value their perspective. Ultimately, you have to make the decision yourself, but input from those who love you most is a valuable data point.

<u>Mentor</u>

If your mentor (as in, someone you respect) gives you advice, listen as objectively as you can, even if you hate what they have to say. What they say may have some nuggets of truth.

<u>Everyone Else</u>

With almost anyone else, listen lightly, nod your head, and smile, but don't rely too heavily either way. Most people project their own fears, expectations, or self-talk onto others. When someone I know tells me they want to be a lion tamer, I might say, "Oh, wow. That's terrifying. I wouldn't do that if I were you." Because I'm not you. And I'm afraid of lions. But that might be exactly what you do best.

## Audience

If your audience speaks, always listen. Who is your audience? Those people you love and feel called to serve. The people you feel drawn to help and improve their lives. Perhaps you haven't found them yet, or maybe you're starting to get an inkling about the people you'd like to spend your time serving. Regardless, if they give you feedback and you want to serve them better, pay attention!

## Inner Voice

If your inner voice speaks, always listen, unless it's negative. That's not your inner voice; it's the world's voice. And the world's voice can often be louder and more insistent. How do you tell the difference? It's tough. But generally speaking, your inner voice sounds affirming, motivating, and inspiring. It will almost never discourage you from doing something unless that thing might bring harm or pain, like walking onto a busy road or jumping off a cliff into murky water. It may also warn you about getting into a bad relationship. But with regard to major and career, expect it to sound like the cheering section at a basketball game. It gives you courage to try new things and explore that idea that has been planted in your soul. On the other hand, the voice of the world plays to the outside/in extrinsic motivators and typically makes you feel ashamed, weak, not good enough.

Not all voices should carry equal weight, so be picky about the advice you listen to (mine included!)

**Fear**

So, once we're armed with all the necessary self-knowledge, why do we ultimately pump the brakes when it comes time to take a step toward our best-fit career or major? The answer to this question alone would merit its own 300-page book, but I'll break it down to one simple word for now: fear.

Fear is the great robber of dreams, the ultimate paralyzer. It appears in many forms, but here are the most pernicious offenders:

1. Fear of Failure:

- What it is: Most fear is this kind. It's a fear of doom and gloom — a fear that you will make the "wrong" decision, people will laugh, and you'll prove to be a massive failure.
- How it manifests: Lots and lots of excuses. "I'd do that, but..." or "the timing's just not right," or "I need to get all my ducks in a row first." It also sounds like "maybe I'm good at this, but there's always someone better" or other variations on "how could I possibly compete?!"
- How you know if you're a victim: You've said, "As soon as I have _____ or _____ happens, then I'll be ready."

2. Fear of Disappointing Others:

- What it is: A debilitating feeling that if you choose a certain path that would otherwise be exciting to you, someone close to you will give you that furrowed brow, shaming look that you can't stand.

- How it manifests: When asked, "How's college?" or "So what are you studying?" you feign excitement and only highlight the classes or possible majors that you know will be pleasing to them.
- How you know if you're a victim: In your last conversation with a family member you said, "I really love my business class (or insert any other class you hate)!" and actually felt sick saying it.

3. Fear of the Unknown:

- What it is: Uncertainty about options, not knowing how it will all turn out, unsure what's "out there."
- How it manifests: Revisiting the same options over and over, unsure which one is "best."
- How you know if you're a victim: You've been considering doing something for a while but keep talking yourself out of it. May also manifest in your roommate, friend, or co-workers saying, "Are you still talking about this?" or "Not this again…"

4. Fear of Financial Insolvency:

- What it is: A fear that you won't make enough to support yourself and the decision will lead you and your family down a dark pit of despair and straight into poverty.
- How it manifests: An excessive focus on needing to know how much you'll make in your new venture. It also may manifest as over-inflating your needs, e.g. "I need at least six figures to make this work."

- How you know if you're a victim: You've said, "I'd love to do it, but what if I don't make any money?" Or you've flat-out blamed money for your risk-aversion — "Yeah, I just don't think I could make it financially."

Fear stops many great people from doing amazing things they would otherwise excel at for a very long time.

## How to Overcome the Fear

A few years ago, I had a memorable phone call with a college student who interviewed me for an assignment. He started by asking if I had any general advice.

Poor guy.

Little did he know that I give advice for a living, and I went on a ten-minute diatribe about the complexities of career.

At the end of the call, he asked me a great question: "What do you dislike most about your job?"

Easy. I can't take it when people won't change. When they won't do something different even when they know they should.

He followed up with an equally profound question: "Why won't people change? And what makes those who do change, change?"

When people change, it's because they've bought into a brighter future than what they currently have that makes it all worth it.

When they won't? It's often because the future I've sold them or they've envisioned isn't bright enough to outweigh the darkness of the fear that holds them back. The enemy of change 100% of the time is fear: fear of failure, of loss, of uncertainty, of judgment, and so on.

When the darkness is darker than the brightness is bright, the trade-off simply isn't worth it to them.

If you're stuck and feel fear about a move you know you should make, try dialing up the brightness on your vision of the future. People with bright visions don't need any pushing — their future pulls them along.

The goal with fear isn't to ignore it. Rather, we should acknowledge it, tip our hat to it, and say, "Thanks. I'll try it anyway." Or just punch it in the face and press on.

Remember, ultimately, when the dust settles, it will be *you* at the desk working the job. Not your parents or siblings, not your mentor or coach, and certainly not the naysayer who says, "You can't make money doing that." And no amount of money — even *that* much — will make the commute home from a job you hate feel better.

Choose fit.

# Chapter 6

## The Three Things You Need to Know

So, we walked through the inside/out model, but I also identified a bazillion things you need to know about yourself to be clear about who you are and to make internally aligned, well-informed decisions. Overwhelming, right? Most people get the power of inside/out, but they wonder what *specifically* they need to know about themselves to get it right.

I have great news.

You really only need to know three things about yourself:

- What you care about. The core beliefs that need to be in play for you to feel fulfilled. We call these **values.**
- What you do best. The God-given abilities that you do better than most other people. These are the foundation of a best-fit major and career. We call these **talents.**
- Where you do your best work. This includes the physical and socioemotional space where you thrive. We call this **environment.**

What I've learned from decades of leading people to best-fit careers and majors is that if they can get clear about three to five bullets under each of those headings, that information is sufficient to make a well-educated decision about whether something is a fit or not. For simplicity, I have clients put that information into what I call a Profile of Self, which is exactly what it sounds like. It's a one-page profile or snapshot of who you are at your best. For example, below is a portion of my profile:

## Values (What I care about)

- Balance — A desire to have a structured schedule that allows equal parts family, work, and personal time.
- Empowerment — Helping others, especially the underdog, to thrive.
- Growth — Potential to constantly improve and develop.

## Talents (What I do best)

- I help individuals synthesize information.
- I prepare a lesson about something relevant to benefit others.
- I facilitate and teach something I care about.
- I research information about a topic that is interesting to me.

## Environments (Where I thrive)

- Frequent interaction with others.
- Opportunity for distraction; working on multiple projects at once.
- Job that allows for big-picture thinking.

Now the question in your mind should be, "Dustin, why *that* information? What makes those three areas special?" I'm glad you asked. This is key.

Conveniently, almost all job descriptions are built the same way, unbeknownst to the people who build them. In other words, HR people craft job descriptions using a formula they don't even recognize, but the formula goes like this:

Job Title

Job Description:

Paragraph 1: Who they are looking for and the things that person would need to care about and believe to work here, also referred to as *values*. I've looked up a general "leadership development" job on Indeed.com and pasted below the sentences from the opening paragraph, bolding the values (and replacing the organization with an "X" — no free advertising of your job posting here!):

At X, we work every day to create products and services that **enrich people's lives**. Our Ad Platforms team is redefining the advertising model by developing highly effective, scalable advertising products that **help [people] thrive** while upholding X's commitment to always **respect user privacy**. We help publishers and developers **promote and monetize their work** while also **helping people around the world discover apps and media**. X is a place where extraordinary people gravitate in order to **do their best work**. Together we craft products and experiences **people once couldn't have imagined** — and now can't imagine living without! If you're excited by the idea of **making a real impact**, and **joining a team where we pride ourselves in being one of the most diverse and inclusive companies in the world**, a career with X might be your dream job!

Do you see it? Values everywhere. If you defined your values in three to five bullets with definitions next to each, then compared those values with this job description, you should be able to see alignment (or lack thereof) clearly.

Paragraph 2: What this individual would need to do well to thrive, usually listed as bullet points. Think *talents*. Again, from the same job posting, below is what they want this person to be able to do well with talents bolded:

- Work closely with Learning and Development and leadership to **create and implement a blended learning curriculum**, including instructor-led, eLearning and resources.
- Support new product launches with **training plans to increase client adoption.**
- **Create product training content** to drive improved sales performance within regional sales teams.
- **Conduct training sessions** to advance both technical and client engagement excellence.
- Work closely with product subject matter experts and champions to **execute consistent and highly effective resources,**
- **Manage and facilitate onboarding training** for regional new hires.
- Integrate scorecard system and staff rotation program to **assess training material quality and delivery effectiveness.**
- **Maintain strategic dashboards and reports** in project management system to highlight key insights in your area of responsibility.

Again, if your talents are of the training, development, management, facilitation, strategy, assessment, and creation variety, this job may be for you.

Paragraph 3: What type of *environment* this person would expect to work in. This includes both the physical space where you do your job and the socio-emotional space, as in the vibe or culture of the organization. Again, from the job description, with environmental factors bolded:

- You'll work under **tight deadlines with minimal supervision in a fast-paced, dynamic environment where quality, creativity, and accountability are tradition**.
- 3-5 years sales/account management training experience in B2B, **tech, or other knowledge-intensive field.**
- Experience developing sales training curriculum for search, media, **technically dense and/or data-oriented products.**
- Experience leading **front-of-the-room trainings** as well as incorporating eLearning for product curriculum across sales and account management teams.
- Proven ability to **juggle multiple projects simultaneously**, capacity to adapt to changing priorities and cut through ambiguity.
- Demonstrate a high **attention to detail and accuracy.**
- **Organized, methodical, and excellent communicator are crucial.**
- Comfortable working closely with high-level executives and key partners

- Experience in the mobile app space, search and/or performance marketing along with **start-up experience** is preferred.

If you like an environment that is fast-paced, changing, detail-oriented, people-focused, in the spotlight, and with multiple projects at once, this is for you! By the way, I was feeling this job description until the environments section. The values and talents were a solid fit, but I couldn't handle the environment, so count me out. I'll stick with Proof Leadership Group.

The idea is that you first build your lens — your Profile of Self — then hold it up against a job description and compare it section by section to look for alignment. What's the threshold we're looking for? It's not an exact science, but I often tell clients if they can find a job where 70% of the description seems to match who they are, they've won the lottery. That's huge! Before even applying, 70% is a fit? Wow. Take the job and run. Then, when you get the job, you can do what's called "job crafting" to make the job you have more of the job you want. It's magic.

Now here's the great news for you. Career and college major descriptions are also full of values, talents, and environments, so the profile serves the same purpose. In fact, if I had read the description below for public relations and compared it to my Profile of Self, I may have majored in something else! Take a look, with values, talents, and environments bolded:

Public relations is a **planned process to influence** public opinion. Most organizations seek to **persuade and build relationships** with various publics to achieve organizational objectives. This emphasis provides opportunities to **write, research, and implement persuasive principles** and **tools of strategic planning** for selected clients.

The Bachelor of Science (BS) degree in Communication with a Public Relations emphasis prepares students for professional work in the public relations industry. Students will learn how to **anticipate, analyze, and interpret public opinion** that can affect the success of business organizations and other entities. In addition to **research**, students will learn how to **influence targeted audiences using persuasive principles and tools to achieve organizational goals**. The use of **traditional and digital media will be accentuated**. Courses in the emphasis are designed to prepare students with **excellent writing skills and other communication skill sets necessary for entering the profession**. (https://www.byui.edu/majors/communication-public-relations.)

Compare that with the sampling of my profile above, and there's not much alignment. Instead, I probably would have majored in Organizational Behavior, which is all about understanding, motivating, rewarding, strengthening, and developing individuals in organizations to help the greater organization get results.

This isn't rocket science, right? It's self-reflection. It's being intentional. It's taking control of your future by choosing options that align with who you are so that you can wake up every morning and get paid, promoted, and rewarded to do what you do best and be who you already are.

So, how do you create your Profile of Self? Step one is to gather data that you can mine to begin to sort out your values, talents, and environments. Let's work through a case study.

## Christina's Story

I want you to play along with me to evaluate a real-life situation as if you were a career coach on my team. I'll tell you the story of a UT Student I coached, and as I describe her predicament, I want you to consider what you would advise. Ready?

"Christina" reached out to me a few years back because I had coached her older brother in college. She was a high school senior here locally in Texas and had been accepted to the University of Texas in Austin. She was thrilled to become a Longhorn but felt stuck regarding her major. Much to her chagrin (and mine), the university was asking her to declare a major before she even arrived on campus (another trend that makes me slap my forehead and merits a 300-page book about why it's a terrible idea), and she felt totally conflicted about what to study. I agreed to meet up with her to talk it through and help her get some clarity.

We arranged a meetup at a local coffee shop, and I got to know her a little before diving into my typical series of questions. I first asked her what she was thinking about declaring as a major.

"Civil engineering," she said with some conviction.

I asked her how she knew that. Like, why *that* major? I had never even heard of civil engineering at her age, and yet she seemed totally confident in her response.

She said she had a math teacher in high school who suggested it. They had done a levee building project that required some mathematical calculations, and her group got an A. Her teacher applauded her contribution and said, "Wow, you should be a civil engineer." And just like that, she was ready to dedicate the next four years (and possibly more) to that major.

By the way, note the outside/in model. She shows some aptitude on a one-time levee-building project in math class, and her teacher makes an off-handed comment about her being a great civil engineer and BAM! She locks onto it.

I asked if she really loved that project, or math for that matter.

"Not really," she said.

Time to explore something new. So, I launched into a litany of questions to get to know her better. I call these the "At Your Best" questions because they give insight into who you are when you're being your best self. You might take a stab at finishing these statements:

- A recent time when I was at my best was . . .
- What I enjoy doing the most is . . .
- My most fulfilling experience was . . .
- The best job or project I ever had was . . .
- The things I like best about myself are . . .
- In all of my schooling, the subjects I thrived the most in were . . .
- List three to five sources you read on a regular basis (magazines, news, blogs, etc.).

- If I surveyed your parents or siblings, your friends, and three to five others who know you well, what would they say you do very best? (If you're not sure, you may choose to ask them and record their responses!)

As she answered these, I took copious notes in my reflection notebook, then reflected her answers back to her. Below is a synopsis of what she shared. This is the part where I want you to play career coach. Assume this is all the information you have about her. What majors would you recommend she explore?

- Loves music because it is a creative outlet.
- Enjoys interacting with people frequently and talking with them.
- Uses empathy to understand others.
- Appreciates flexibility and freedom to innovate.
- She is good at ideating and visualizing outcomes.
- She can easily see connections.
- Her favorite class was English because of the opportunities to interact with people.
- In her free time she listens to motivational speeches, like TED talks.
- She loves working on a team of people and building relationships.
- Her favorite experience in high school was visiting an orphanage and talking to people about their experiences.

So, what would you recommend? Typically, when I share this story, audiences might exclaim, "Sociology!" or "English!" or "Psychology!" Or music, education, social work, organizational behavior, or any other number of socially-focused majors. I shared the same thing with her, then pulled out my phone and Googled "civil engineering." Here's what it said:

Civil engineers design, construct, supervise, operate, and maintain large construction projects and systems, including roads, buildings, airports, tunnels, dams, bridges, and systems for water supply and sewage treatment.

Wait, what? Look at what she does best, then look at the definition of civil engineering. Do you see it? I'll wait.

You're right. It's not a fit. Now, a few caveats, especially for those civil engineers out there who are reacting to my assumptions: first, I'm sure civil engineering needs people just like her in their industry, so if she wanted to make a run at it, she could potentially thrive. Also, I get that this is a simplified definition of civil engineering. Blah blah blah. However, just based on a super simple flyover of what the career is and who she is, one can see that there may be better options out there. So why start off college picking something that may not fit? Why spend four years and tens of thousands of dollars to study something that is painful? Or rather, why not start by picking something that might at least be in the right arena?

Well, I shared this with her, and I could see the wheels spinning. We closed the conversation, and I encouraged her to go search out some majors that played to her strengths of empathy, building relationships, connecting with people, motivation, inspiration, and telling a story.

A few months later, I got a note from her. She had declared her major:

Civil engineering.

(Womp womp.)

But she also shared this, emphasis added:

Although I've only been in school for a few months, it **feels as if I've been in school forever**; in fact, it feels like I have been staring at formulas and numbers nonstop for the past few weeks. I find myself asking, **'Where are the genuine people interactions?'** or **'What about connecting with others over our enthusiasm for life and all the great things we can do to make this world better?'** I find myself asking questions of this sort many times throughout the week, and I begin to wonder if I'm either overthinking engineering or I simply just don't enjoy it. I know my inner voice is telling me exactly what I know deep down inside. **I know that my heart is just not in engineering.**

I replied:

Thanks for the update. In re-reading my notes from our brief convo, here is what I had written down about you:

[Insert the notes I wrote on what she said previously.]

Are you seeing what I'm seeing? Or rather, are you noticing what's not there?

I don't see strong correlation between what you value and what you do well and engineering. Now, I'm not proposing that you bail on engineering, but if I were in your shoes, here's what I would do:

1. Get involved in student organizations and events that reinforce what you love to do. If anything, these might give you the confidence to make a leap to pursuing something more aligned full-time.

2. Take some classes in the spring outside of engineering, particularly in psychology, sociology, or business. Even just one.

3. Identify people on campus who seem to be teaching or doing something that interests you and get to know them. Learn about their career path, ask about future career options for someone from that field, and immerse yourself.

4. When the time is right, make the leap! Listen to your inner voice, Christina. It won't steer you wrong. The most telling line of the whole email was this one: "I know that my heart is just not in engineering." Done and done. Time to do something else! Reduce the number of classes you're taking in engineering and ramp up the other classes. You don't need to officially declare a new major just yet, but you can begin to explore and minimize the time you're wasting in a major that's not interesting to you.

If you had to pick another major right now, right this moment, what would you pick? Don't overthink it — you probably have an inclination for what it might be...you don't need to have the next ten years figured out. Just take it a step at a time.

Listen to your inner voice and suppress the voice of resistance. The former will lead you to a passion, the latter to a ball-and-chain job.

Keep me posted on what you do next. I'd love to stay connected.

Dustin

I sent off that note, and she replied with a short message of gratitude and that was it. No word.

Four years later, Christina graduated. Any guess what she graduated in?

Civil engineering.

Now before you guffaw and throw your hands in the air, we've all been there. I know I have been. Why did she stay the course, knowing it wasn't a fit? Who knows. Parents, societal pressures, money, college advisors…any number of extrinsic factors could be at play.

In reality, though, the root of all of these is simple: fear. Fear of disappointing others or herself, fear of financial insolvency, fear of you-name-it. I've included this example because I want you to know that fear comes into the picture for everybody at some point or another. That's why I called it out in the previous chapter. I want you to be able to recognize the fear for what it is. Fear is the great crippler, the one thing that will hold you back unless you decide now that you are committed to prioritizing fit and making an inside/out decision, no matter the cost. The process takes effort, but remember Emily and Trent's stories. The effort is worth the rewards.

The most important step is reflection. If you are going to make an inside/out decision, it starts with getting clear about what's on the *inside*. In the following chapters, I want to take you through that process using several examples and some of the key protocols and questions I use to guide a client through self-discovery.

# Chapter 7

## Step One - Reflect

When I first meet with a client to help them get clear about who they are, I always follow the same process. After only an hour, we get a really good idea of where they might fit based on intrinsic factors: values, talents, and environments. In fact, as I go through this with them, I'll often mark the values, talents, and environments as we go, although for your purposes the simple reflection may be sufficient.

Let me say that again: you don't need to be a trained and practiced career coach and tabulate and differentiate the values, talents, and environments as you go. Don't overthink this. The reflection is what we're after.

The first part of the client meeting is dedicated to the **past**. Your purpose lies in your past, not your future. Purpose isn't something "out there" waiting to be stumbled upon. Rather, it emerges from the experiences in your past that have shaped who you are today. In fact, I typically find that where you fit today is often the result of a series of "hints" and "clues" along the way.

To surface that pattern of hints and clues, I lead clients through a series of questions that go something like this:

- Where are you from?
- How many siblings do you have, and what number are you?

- How did your family dynamics influence you at a young age?
- How did the place you grew up shape you?
- What did you think about doing when you grew up? Like, when people would ask what you wanted to do for a career, what did you say, no matter how ridiculous it seems now?
- What subjects and activities did you thrive in? Why?
- What was the best project you ever did in school and why?
- What did you do when you weren't in the classroom? What hobbies were you drawn to?
- What would people in your student organizations, classes, or other extracurriculars say you did best?
- What did you most enjoy?
- What did you like to read? Listen to?
- When did you first notice one of your talents? What happened, and what was it?
- Who did you look up to and in what ways?
- What did you daydream about?
- When you graduated from high school and started thinking about college, what did you imagine you might be doing?

The key is to answer these in depth. Spare no detail. The more information you capture, the more likely you are to mine out the clues that will help you on your search. By the way, I've never been successful answering these questions in isolation and mining out my purpose. There's something powerful about making this a conversation, so ask your best friend, a family member, or significant other to go out to dinner with you and interview you. Find someone who is naturally curious and asks great follow-up questions to press you for in-depth answers    .

What are you searching for? It's not the questions that hold power or even the answers in and of themselves. Just because you loved the Ninja Turtles as a kid doesn't mean you should be a ninja. It's what those answers reveal *about* you — the pattern — that matters. At the risk of giving away the power of the exercise, when I interview a client, I'm listening for some key phrases:

- I like…
- I love…
- I'm good at…
- I have a knack for…
- I do _____ best…
- I feel energized by…
- I have an ability to…

Why? Because these phrases almost always precede **values, talents, and ideal environments.** They show aptitudes, energy, and purpose. What follows these phrases are clues that the inner self is begging the outer self to piece together into a meaningful picture of the future. I mentioned before that I capture these things and often ask clients to expound on them, listening for three things and labeling them as I go:

- Values — words and phrases about things that are important. Examples:

  o   I need to **feel like I'm making a difference.** (V)

- o   I like **directing my own work on a daily basis**. (V)

- o   I value **flexibility**. (V)

- Talents — words or phrases that sound like action phrases. Examples:

  - o   I love **telling people small things they can do to be better.** (T)

  - o   I have knack for **identifying the bottleneck in a system** or room for potential that people aren't tapping into. (T)

  - o   I'm good at **synthesizing information** to make the complex more simple. (T)

- Environments — words or phrases that describe a physical space or socio-emotional space (i.e. vibe) needed to thrive.

  - o   I love **detail-oriented, meticulous** work. (E)

  - o   I love **being on the go**, always moving. (E)

  - o   I like **predictability** in my schedule. (E)

Let me give an example.

Recently I talked with my good friend, Cade. Cade is a tremendous leader and was just beginning his college experience when we talked. He is the kind of young person who makes you think, "This guy's got it all figured out. He's got it together!" And yet, Cade felt totally lost. He didn't even feel like he had an inkling about what he might pursue in college and beyond. So, we set up a time to hop on the phone and see what we could figure out in an hour.

I started by letting him know that his only job on the call was to talk. I'd ask the questions, and he would tell stories. I would also capture what I heard and share it with him. I'm using his example now with his permission, hoping it might be instructive to you.

I asked him to take me back as far as he could remember and to tell me his story. As we did with Christina, play career counselor with me for this exercise. What would you recommend he explore? Below are the key bullets I captured with a few of my follow-up questions in parentheses:

- Grew up in Herriman, Utah
- Family of seven kids, my twin and I right in the middle
- My dad passed when I was 12
- Loved to play sports, soccer my whole life, snowboarding. (What did you love about sports?)

    o Love being somewhere with people who have a desire to be better and improve (V)

    o People who have drive, working towards something (V)

    o Can't be around people who lack vision (E)

    o Working with others to do something hard — being part of a team (V)

- Love being outside, adventures, hikes and things
- Love family activities; Mom loved to travel
- Everyone pulled together when my dad passed away
- Took ballroom and hip-hop class, peer tutoring classes, woodworking (What did you love about those?)

- o Like doing hands-on work (E)
- o Something new and different every day (E)
- o When I have a clear task, determined to do it (T)
- I love being able to help people, serving other people (T) (Why?)
  - o Grateful for the help they received
  - o The satisfaction
  - o Drawn to help people that have a desire to be better but something's holding them back (T); especially people with special needs

I then asked him what he thinks he does best. While he was growing up, what did he learn    about his talents? And, if I were to ask his friends or family about what he does best, what would they say? Here's what he said:

- Genuine (T)
- Working with people (T)
- Peacemaker (T)
- Determined to accomplish something (T)

I also asked him to fast forward ten years. He's in his dream job. What does he *see*, even if he's not sure what it's called?

- Dream job: Married, family, solid house, beautiful place — be on an adventure every day (V)
- Meet new people each day, hands on (E)

- Money — want a balance of loving my job and making money, even if it means not making as much money. (What do your parents do for a living?)
  - o Mom is a nurse, stepdad does IT stuff, Dad was in sales
- Ministering to people (T) — noticing when someone is unsure and helping them
- Creating an environment where people don't feel judged (T)

After exploring the past, I like to guide the client through a few different exercises. The first I call the <u>Whiteboard Scenario</u>. It goes like this:

If I invited you into a room with a whiteboard at the front and 30 seats filled with a captive audience and gave you 60 minutes to teach three 20-minute lectures **with no preparation,** what do you know so well and feel so passionate about that you could teach it?

Try it now. What would *you* teach? Remember: no prep. Captive audience with notebooks out. Get over the fear and trepidation you would feel and focus on what's so deep in your soul or what you know enough about **and are passionate about** that you could teach it. Here's what Cade said:

1. The basics of pickleball and how to play the sport (T).
2. How to find joy through loving other people; how to be there for each other; community (V).
3. How to work hard and stay focused. If I get a task, I'm determined to do it. Work hard in whatever situation (T).

Again, what I'm looking for are patterns. He's obviously drawn toward building community and teaching others determination. I would answer these questions very differently, as would you. We each have our niche, our areas of expertise. Mine would be how to invest, how to find a meaningful career, and how to build a team. How about you?

Next, I walked him through the Arena Exercise. It goes like this:

Pretend for a moment that you are on a street corner with two large arenas, one on each corner across from one another. One arena is the "Thing" arena. If you buy a ticket and enter this arena, you'll spend your career working with *things*. Think: engineers, accountants, construction workers, etc. Even though the ultimate goal of the things might be to benefit humans, you're actually working with things — widgets, inanimate objects, numbers — each day. Some doctors may even fit in this arena, such as a radiologist who reads images or even a heart surgeon who might have some pre- and post-op interaction with a patient but who spends most of their time working with the actual heart — a thing. More "thing" professions might include dentistry, data science, IT, physics, archaeology, and so forth.

The other arena is the "People" arena. In this arena, your beginning and end product is people. You spend your day-to-day efforts studying people, talking with people, and working with people directly. Think: psychologists, trainers, coaches, teachers, therapists, salespeople, sociologists, social workers, physical therapists, etc. Again, it's not a perfect metaphor, and there is certainly some overlap between the two arenas, but you get the gist. The People arena focuses on…people.

Which one would you go in?

For Cade, the answer was clear, and you could have guessed it from the notes above. He loves people — interacting with them, teaching them, building them up and strengthening them. He's a community guy. No brainer.

The second question:

Now that you've entered an arena, choose your seat. If you sit on the floor, you're doing hands-on, practical work. For the Thing arena, this might be actually working with the hammer or tightening the screws or manipulating the data. In the People arena, this means being knee-to-knee and eye-to-eye with the humans, like a teacher, coach, or therapist.

If you're in the upper level, you are analyzing patterns and disseminating information to help those on the floor. For the Thing arena, this might be an economist who analyzes patterns and disseminates information to day traders or wealth managers or government officials. Or a physicist who researches the way worlds interact and shares that with engineers or rocket scientists. (I'm clearly out of my lane here.) For the People arena, this might be the sociologist or psychologist who publishes research to guide the teacher, or the organizational consultant who surveys teams to understand their culture and passes that information along to the coach or manager who uses it to guide their interactions. Which level are you sitting in?

Again, for Cade, he said he's definitely on the bottom level:

- Definitely People arena; I'm drawn to the bottom level.
- I get energy from talking to people (E).
- I love interacting with people, love preparing myself to interact (E).

Where would you end up? People or Thing arena? And at what level of seat? On the ground actually doing the work with the person or widget? Or higher up observing the patterns, data, interactions, and documenting, analyzing, and/or writing about it?

Finally, I guided him through the <u>Consultant Exercise</u>. In this thought exercise, I asked him to pretend that he and I were co-owners of a career coaching agency. We would receive nothing more than a profile of someone, and our job was to read the profile and recommend a few possible majors or career paths based on the information given. I went back through my coded notes, quickly copied and pasted them into the format below, and shared these values, talents, and environments with Cade as if I were describing a random person. Again, these are the notes I already captured above, just in a more streamlined format:

**Values**

- Self-improvement and growth
- Drive
- Community
- Challenge

## Talents

- Breaking down projects into specific tasks
- Working hard in any situation
- Accomplishing tasks with determination
- Being genuine with people
- Being a peacemaker by creating harmony and resolving conflict
- Helping people; serving them
- Helping people who have a desire to improve, but are challenged by a limiting factor
- Helping people with special needs.

## Environments

- Hands-on work
- Something new and different every day
- Can't be around people who lack vision
- Meet new people each day
- Learning, preparing, then applying

I then asked Cade to share at least three possible career paths. If he had to suggest a few areas to explore that might align with this individual's profile, what would they be? What would *you* recommend? Here's what he and I came up with when we combined our ideas:

- Coaching
- Mentoring
- Teaching
- Education
- Seminary

- Nonprofit Management
- Business Management, Organization Behavior
- Human Capital Consulting
- Trainer
- Counselor/Therapist
- Construction Manager
- Special Education

This is a powerful exercise. See, I believe that many people already have an idea of what they might like to do, but the extrinsic forces are so strong that they deny those options. This gives the client an opportunity to share what's deep in the recesses of their mind, rooted in information and reflected back to them about who they are. I'm always interested to see what makes the list, and usually find that the direction they head in is something they had considered all along.

Cade was no different.

I asked if any of those jumped out to him. He thought for a moment, then said, "Yeah. Special Education." I'll be honest, I didn't expect that. Teaching maybe. Or training. But where did Special Ed come from? I did hear one tiny mention of it at the beginning of our call that I never pursued but didn't hear it manifest almost any other time. You could see it up above when I asked about his past, and the last thing he said was, "Drawn to help people that have a desire to be better but something's holding them back, *especially people with special needs.*"

This was a pivotal moment in our coaching conversation. I asked him to share more about why and how that made the list. He lit up and said that his mom was always involved in helping children with special needs. He often had opportunities to work with these kids, *teaching them skills, helping them focus and work hard, building their confidence, and helping them feel like they belong.* He used to teach sports in combination with special education and loved the feeling of *breaking down challenging tasks into more doable actions.* And he got to teach various things he knows something about: communication, sports, working hard, focus, and setting and achieving goals.

Whaaa…? Where did this come from, and why didn't it come up earlier? I asked him this, and he simply said he wasn't sure. It just didn't. The truth is, each of us has inspired ideas about our future, but we suppress them for whatever reason. Usually that reason is fear, and this may have subconsciously been the case; maybe fear of disapproval from others or fear of being able to make it work financially. In reality, it doesn't matter why we suppress those feelings, as long as we come back to them and let them live, judgment-free, at least long enough to move to Step Two: Exploration.

Reflection is the key. Don't shortchange this process. Once you've surfaced some core self-learning, now and *only now* are you prepared to explore all the possibilities. In fact, I call the next two steps the twin engines of career searching: exploration and connecting.

**TAKE ACTION:** Before moving on, take some time to answer the questions in this chapter, beginning with the At Your Best questions, then moving through the various exercises below. After answering the questions as organically as you can, go back with a pen or highlighter and look for the values, talents, and environments you need to be your best self, then roll these together into the beginnings of a Profile of Self. As mentioned earlier, you may find it easier to pair up with a close friend, family member, or mentor to have them ask you the questions and press you for answers. Reflection in isolation can be challenging!

## 1. At Your Best

Complete these statements in as much detail as possible. Use paragraphs, not phrases. You might try finishing the sentence, then answering the question "why?" For example, when was a recent time you were at your best and *why* were you at your best?

- A recent time when I was at my best was . . .
- What I enjoy doing the most is . . .
- My most fulfilling experience was . . .
- The best job or project I ever had was . . .
- The things I like best about myself are . . .
- In all of my schooling, the subjects I thrived the most in were . .
- List 3-5 sources you read on a regular basis (magazines, news, blogs, etc.).
- If I surveyed your parents or siblings, your friends, and three to five others who know you well, what would they say you do very best? (If you're not sure, you may choose to ask them and record their responses!)

## 2. Explore the Past

- Where are you from?
- How many siblings do you have, and what number are you?
- How did your family dynamics influence you at a young age?
- How did the place you grew up shape you?
- What did you think about doing when you grew up? Like, when people would ask what you wanted to do for a career, what did you say, no matter how ridiculous it seems now?
- What subjects and activities did you thrive in? Why?
- What did you do when you weren't in the classroom? What hobbies were you drawn to?
- What would people in your student organizations, classes, or other extracurriculars say you did best?
- What did you most enjoy?
- What did you like to read? Listen to?
- When did you first notice one of your talents? What happened, and what was it?
- Who did you look up to and in what ways?
- What did you daydream about?
- When you graduated from high school and started thinking about college, what did you imagine you might be doing?

## 3. Whiteboard Scenario

If I invited you into a room with a whiteboard at the front and 30 seats filled with a captive audience and gave you 60 minutes to teach three 20-minute lectures **with no preparation,** what do you know so well and feel so passionate about that you could teach it?

## 4. Arena Exercise

People or Thing?

Low seat or high?

## 5. Consultant Exercise

Get out of yourself, float up above the room, and be objective. Suppress the extrinsic pressures! Based on what you see above, what are three options this person should explore?

# Chapter 8

## Step Two - Explore

Trivia time! How many college majors are there in the world? Don't cheat and look it up. Just take a wild guess.

30?

120?

Try *1,800*, according to mymajors.com. Eighteen hundred different directions you could go!

How about careers?

2,000?

5,000?

Careerplanner.com has identified more than 12,000 different careers.

Okay, last one. How many jobs are currently open? As of the writing of this book and the most recent search on indeed.com, there are 3,396,546 jobs in the U.S. alone. Almost 3.5 million.

That's mind-blowing. As humans, we are notoriously bad at estimating. Think of the last time you guessed the number of pennies in a jar or M&Ms in a can. You probably weren't even close. Why does this matter? Because this same thing happens with jobs, careers, and majors, and it's a major problem, no pun intended. We tend to dramatically underestimate the number of options we have available to us, instead cramming ourselves into one of only a *few*. As I often tell my     clients, there is a hiring manager somewhere in the world today looking for someone just like you, but they don't know you exist or where to find you, and you didn't even know the job they are trying to fill was a possibility. Incredible!

When we look back at the outside/in model, notice the number of circles the stick figure is trying to decide between: four.

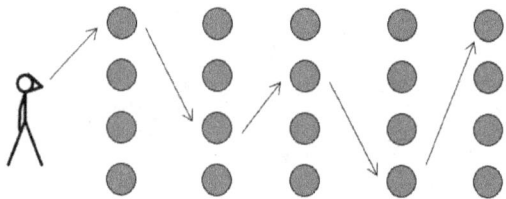

That's not by accident. What I've found time and again as I coach college students on identifying a major or professionals on changing jobs is that they are typically only aware of and choosing between about four industries: business, education, medicine, and engineering. *Some* may add a fifth in law. Why is that? Why are we so narrow in our exploration, especially when there are almost 2,000 options?

Again, the answer lies in our natural tendency to prefer less options to more. More options create more opportunities for stress, heartache, and "wrong" decisions. Fewer options reduce the risk and simplify decision-making for our brains. Plus, we have dramatically oversimplified life and happiness down to "study business, get a job, make lots of money, be happy," replacing "business" with whichever of the five majors we were told will help us succeed in life. This, of course, is a false paradigm, but a dominant one in society, nonetheless. We only consider a few options because those are the only ones we know are out there. The trouble is that you don't know what you don't know! There is a major out there specifically for you, but you likely don't even know it exists.

That's where exploration comes in.

The goals of exploration are threefold:

1.  **Expand your options**. Before you begin to narrow down to a best-fit major, you need to know what's out there. You need options! Diverging is the creative process of exploring, expanding options, and considering lots of possibilities. Converging is narrowing in on one option, consolidating choices, and making a decision. Before converging, diverge and generate options.

2.  **Gather information**. You don't just need options; you need at least an elementary understanding of what each option is. For example, what do you think of when I say "psychologist?" Lying on a couch discussing your personal problems with a stranger? Wrong. Psychology prepares you for everything from consulting to pre-med and from marketing to leadership. We must get past what we *think* a major is and gather enough meaningful information to make an informed decision.

3.  **Hone your search**. Exploration follows a process I call scramble and stick. You spend the first half of exploration searching out everything under the sun that could be a potential fit based on who you are, then begin narrowing down your search to the two to three options that seem most likely to align with who you are. It looks something like this:

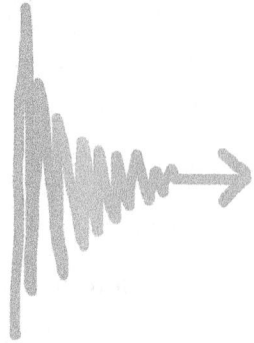

One quick note about what exploration *isn't*. **This is *not* the stage to decide on your major or career.** This is only Step Two. Before you can make a truly informed decision, you'll need to Connect in Step Three and use effective decision-making to make a choice. We're getting there, but let me show you the three easiest and most effective methods for exploring options:

1. The Strategic Google Search
2. The Career Search
3. The Major Search

**The Strategic Google Search**

The first thing most people do when they can't figure out what to do with their life is to open Google and search — you guessed it — "what should I do with my life?"

As if Google is a genie that can divine the ultimate life purpose.

The problem here is that people lack a lens to screen the options. Google makes a bazillion suggestions but you don't have a method for sorting through them to decide if one is better than the other. In other words, everything looks the same. How do you determine whether something is more of a fit than something else? Gut instinct? However, when the correct search terms are applied, Google and its masterful algorithm become that genie and can surface, like magic, career options that fit surprisingly well.

The correct search terms I'm referring to are your **values, talents, and environments** from the Reflection section in Step One. And the method for using those search terms is deceptively simple:

1. Open Google.
2. Enter two to three of your Talent words or statements plus...
3. The word "jobs," plus...
4. A geographic location
5. Press **Enter** (aka rub the genie lamp) and wait with bated breath.

For example, I was working with a client recently with these talents:

- Building relationships of trust with people to be responsive to their needs.
- Planning, organizing, and executing an idea to make it happen.
- Getting things done.
- Coming up with creative ideas that haven't been done before.
- Motivating others to keep them on track.

We opened Google on our coaching call and inserted the following search terms in the box, separated by commas:

Building relationships, planning, organizing, motivating others, jobs, Houston

Several sites popped up with more than 20 jobs each that had those search terms. Try it now to see an example of what we saw. Our next string of terms was slightly different:

Building relationships, executing ideas, motivating others, jobs, Houston

And sure enough, the search returned different results with lots of new options that fit, including an Assistant Vice President of Alumni Relations, a Merchandising Execution Manager, and Executive Customer Success Manager. The common themes between each? Building relationships, executing ideas, and motivating others!

Again, it's deceptively simple.

Once you've returned results, then what? You should spend no less than two to three hours reading job descriptions looking for a fit. As shared at the beginning, look for connections between your Profile of Self and the job description.

Once you find a description that seems to fit, scroll down to the latter half of the description and search for a subhead that says something like "Education/Experience Needed." What you are looking for is the type of degree and corresponding majors that fit the job. For example, the Assistant Vice President of Alumni Relations says a bachelor's degree with experience in strategic planning, leadership, partnership-building, and/or philanthropy would be a baseline expectation. Now you have something to guide your major search. We'll do more of this in the Major Search in a moment, but you could likely major in Communications, Non-profit Management, or Finance and be solid.

By the way, how do you know if the job is a fit? Don't overthink this. If it looks interesting, ignites something internally, and you get a rush of endorphins, flag it. Then backtrack the education section to figure out what you'd need to study to eventually get there. Also, what level of job are you looking for? Again, it doesn't matter. It could be something entry-level or something you'll qualify for ten years into the future. The reason it doesn't matter is that none of these jobs will be available when you graduate in one year or four years anyway. And a lot will happen between now and then. You're simply trying to position yourself in the right "arena."

That's it! Give it a try and see what comes up.

## The Career Search

The second option for narrowing your search is to focus on *careers* instead of *jobs*. In the Strategic Google Search, we're exploring among those three million jobs available in the United States. That can be overwhelming. The Career Search seeks to narrow down your options from the 12,000 available by using a powerful search engine called Career One Stop (careeronestop.org), sponsored by the U.S. Department of Labor. No, I'm not getting a kickback from the government for lauding their site. You should know they're too cheap for that.

What I love about this site is that each career comes with a description that aligns surprisingly well with the Profile of Self and a one to two-minute video that shows a "day in the life" of that career. You can really get a feel for what the career entails, all from the comfort of your sofa.

The search method here is simple. Navigate to careeronestop.org/videos, click on "Career Videos" on the left-hand side, then select a "cluster." For example, I've chosen "Education and Training" and the dropdown arrow reveals about 75 different careers in that field, from "Adapted Physical Education Specialist" down to "Tutor." If you select one, the page reveals a short description, a video, the average salary on the left sidebar, a career outlook below that (sunny for Adapted PE Specialists!), and the type of degree (in this case, Bachelor's). If you click "Learn More," it displays schools with that major and…this is key…program names. It turns out a degree in "Special Education and Teaching" will get the job done!

Boom. You've "backtracked" the career to narrow down the major.

Easy as that. I challenge you to spend a few hours searching through careers and narrowing down two to three that look promising, then backtrack the major to look for the program name. And pay attention to sunny skies (but don't let a cloudy outlook shake your trajectory). Remember, you're not trying to narrow it down to just one at this stage. Your goal is to discover several options that would logically fit for you, given what you know about yourself.

**The Major Search**

I've saved the best for last. On every college website or in any college academic catalog, each major has a description to help a searcher determine fit. And, as with the job description example at the beginning of the book, every major description is essentially written the same way — as a series of values, talents, and environments phrases.

The goal here is to take what you've discovered in the first two searches and really start to home in on two to three best-fit majors. Let's look at a few examples.

You can search majors from a university website or you can use a general website such as princetonreview.com/college-major-search to begin surfacing majors. In this case, I've searched "Mechanical Engineering" and below is the overview of the major:

"Diversity" is the key word when it comes to Mechanical Engineering. There are many fields in which Mechanical engineering plays a role: automated manufacturing, environmental control, transportation, biomedical fields, computer fields, fossil fuel and nuclear power…the list goes on and on. Mechanical Engineers are concerned with imagining and implementing programs and devices that improve our world and our movement in it. A Mechanical Engineering major's designing endeavors are diverse, from tiny measuring instruments to huge aircraft carriers or power plants. They also are involved with testing, evaluating, distributing, and marketing the devices they and their colleagues create.

If all of these challenges appeal to you, Mechanical Engineering might be a major to consider. As with other engineering programs, your course of study may include one or more semesters of a co-operative education program, in which you will be employed full-time with an appropriate company. A co-operative is a great way to put your knowledge to use, and often your co-op job leads to post-graduation employment.

At first glance, this seems like a broad description of a general major. But with the insight we have about values, talents, and environments, you can start to see that the phrases they use matter. Using a highlighter or underlining phrases with a pen, pay attention to the "type" of person who fits this major. I've done the dirty work for you on this one:

**"Diversity" is the key word** when it comes to Mechanical Engineering. There are **many fields** in which Mechanical engineering plays a role: automated manufacturing, environmental control, transportation, biomedical fields, computer fields, fossil fuel and nuclear power…the list goes on and on. Mechanical Engineers are concerned with **imagining and implementing programs and devices that improve our world and our movement in it**. A Mechanical Engineering major's designing endeavors are diverse, from tiny measuring instruments to huge aircraft carriers or power plants. They also are involved with **testing, evaluating, distributing, and marketing** the devices they and their colleagues create.

If all of these challenges appeal to you, Mechanical Engineering might be a major to consider. As with other engineering programs, your course of study may include one or more semesters of a co-operative education program, in which you will be employed full-time with an appropriate company. A co-operative is a great way to put your knowledge to use, and often your co-op job leads to post-graduation employment.

People who are talented in testing, evaluating, distributing, and marketing and who thrive on variety, imaginative spaces, and implementation would do well here. Is that you? If not, keep searching.

Try this one on your own: Developmental Psychology. Highlight or underline the words and phrases that describe the type of person who would thrive. What do you see?

Psychology is a huge field, and it's no wonder. Anytime a discipline has as its focus something as monumentally broad as the study of behavior, you had better expect a whole lot of concentrations and specializations.

Somewhere in that long list of psychology majors is Developmental Psychology. Just like a general psychology major, Developmental Psychology is concerned with human behavior. As a specialized major, it is intended for the brave man or woman who is looking to put their education into direct practice and use after graduation.

As a Developmental Psychology major, you'll be prepared to work as a psychologist with a wide number of different populations, including children, the elderly, and families. Many developmental psychologists work directly with one or more of these groups, focusing on the causes and reasons behind behavior.

Do you see what I see? You would do well in this major if you are interested in why people do what they do, like direct practice (as in face-to-face, direct work with people every day), and are drawn to serve a certain population, be it children, the elderly, or families. And this is only based on three paragraphs. You can find longer major descriptions, videos, and more to get an in-depth feel for this major and your potential fit.

Doing a Major Search is the purest way to search for fit, using the Profile of Self as confirmation.

By the way, circling back to Cade's story, there is one other way to do a Major Search. Remember at the end of the Consultant Exercise I asked Cade to brainstorm with me a handful of majors that might fit based on the information we mined. He came up with several, but ultimately doubled back to Special Education. I asked him what university he was attending (Utah Valley University) and then Googled "Utah Valley University Special Education Major" which took me right to "Special Education" in the School of Education. The description wasn't too helpful:

The Professional Special Education Teacher Education Program at Utah Valley University is designed to prepare quality, entry-level candidates for teaching students with mild to moderate disabilities in special education programs grades K-12. Students successfully completing the Teacher Education Program graduation and licensure requirements will receive a BS in Special Education and a Level I Utah Professional Teaching License.

However, we did look at the classes required for the degree and several of those spoke to him.

So, we tried a different approach. I Googled "Special Education Career Path" and got a hit from bestcolleges.com that said this under the "Why Choose a Career in Special Education?":

Many people find helping students with special needs fulfilling and rewarding. Teachers use their instructional skills, understanding of child development, and creative talents to find new ways to share information and help their students grow and succeed.

Careers in special education require skills related to instructing, coordinating activities, and active listening. Classroom teachers work with administrators, counselors, other teachers, and parents or guardians to develop individual learning plans. These plans outline academic accommodations, learning goals, and behavioral goals.

Communication, patience, and resourcefulness top the list of qualities that prospective special education teachers should possess. They also need interpersonal skills to work with other educators and build positive relationships with parents and students.

I know it's a few pages back, but if you look at what Cade does best, this description is *him*. Using instructional skills and creative talents to find new ways to share information? Instructing, coordinating activities, and active listening? Setting goals and plans, using communication, and building relationships? Holy smokes. Direct hit.

And yet, lest we stop there, I also took his interest in hiking and being outdoors and combined that with education to look at the major "Exercise Science and Outdoor Recreation" at UVU. The description:

In addition to a strong background in recreation theory, experiential education, outdoor leadership, risk management and program planning, graduates of this program leave with a proficiency in a variety of both land and water-based skill acquisition courses, such as avalanche awareness, whitewater kayaking and backpacking. More than preparation for a career in the outdoor field, the major in Outdoor Recreation Management grooms students for a lifetime of outdoor participation and leadership.

And when I looked up jobs in this field, I got a hit for "12 Dream Outdoor Recreation and Conservation Careers" that knocked him out of his seat. As we read descriptions and analyzed college major paths, he lit up.

It's amazing to think that after one hour of self-reflection and a bit of exploration online, he went from "I have no idea" to needing to be in a people-oriented, human service field, likely education, exercise science and outdoor recreation, psychology, sociology, human resource management, communication or some other type of collaborative field. We also discovered this sweet degree path: "Applied Communication" (https://www.uvu.edu/comm/degrees.html) which prepares you for education, training, consulting, etc. If I could go back in time and try again, I would have majored in this!

Public relations. Sheesh. SMH.

Step Two is all about exploration and surfacing options that make sense for you as an individual. **Again, this isn't the phase to narrow your choices.** Your whole goal is divergence, which is to expand your options and discover what you don't know.

Most people have no problem doing Step Two because it's safe, easy, and comfortable. You can do it in your pajamas. But remember, it's only one of the "twin engines" of choosing a college major or career path. Don't stop short or your plane will lack power and balance. In the next chapter we will look at the other engine of identifying a best-fit major: Connecting.

**TAKE ACTION:** It's time to explore! Somewhere out there are a major, a career, and a job that fit perfectly with your unique combination of values, talents, and environments. Now, and only *now,* are you allowed to open that Google browser and search "careers in _____." Why? Because now you know what you're looking for — a career that maximizes your best self. The Profile becomes your lens to guide your career search.

Exploration to discover your best-fit major and career is a **three-step process.** Don't skip steps! Work through the process *in order* for best results.

**STEP 1: Search Jobs**

Start broad by searching for potential jobs that align with you and your Profile of Self. Follow these steps:

1. Open Google.
2. Insert two to three of your Talent words and phrases from your Profile of Self.
3. Add the word "jobs."
4. Add a geographic location, e.g., "United States" or "Florida" or "Memphis." Start broad by searching for the whole country, then narrow to places you might want to live.

Example: building relationships, strategy, communication, jobs, Houston

Example: creating, organizing, developing, jobs, Miami

1. Scan jobs, looking for job descriptions that sound interesting. Once you find one, compare it to your Profile of Self. Does it align? If so, insert the link below to save it. If not, move on and keep looking.

Your goal is to identify two to three diverse jobs that look interesting. Then scan the "Education/Background" section at the bottom of the job description for clues about the type of degree and ideal majors that fit that job. Add that information below.

**Job 1:** _____

What education does this job require? (e.g., amount of education, degree type, and relevant majors):

_____

_____

_____

_____

_____

**Job 2:** _____

What education does this job require? (e.g., amount of education, degree type, and relevant majors):

_____

_____

_____

_____

_____

**Job 3:** _____

What education does this job require? (e.g., amount of education, degree type, and relevant majors):

_____

_____

_____

_____

_____

## STEP 2: Search Careers

Next, search for ideal careers, again based on your Profile of Self. Follow the steps below:

1. Go to careeronestop.org/videos

2. If you have careers you know you want to explore, type them in the search bar at the top of the page. Otherwise, scan through careers by clicking "Career Videos" on the left column, then scanning through the various careers that look interesting.

3. When you find a career that piques your interest, copy and paste the link below. In addition, watch the career video, then look at the left column on the career page to "Learn More" about education. Note the majors that are suggested on that page.

**Career 1:** _____

What education is recommended? (e.g., amount of education, degree type, and relevant majors):

_____

_____

_____

_____

_____

**Career 2:** _____

What education is recommended? (e.g., amount of education, degree type, and relevant majors):

_____

_____

_____

_____

_____

**Career 3:** _____

What education is recommended? (e.g., amount of education, degree type, and relevant majors):

_____

_____

_____

_____

_____

**STEP 3: Search Majors**

With a good understanding of interesting jobs and careers, you are now prepared to search majors to see what might be a good fit. Your goal is to surface two to three good options for majors based on the profile you've developed. Follow the instructions below and fill out the templates beginning on the next page for three majors that look interesting:

1. First, go to princetonreview.com/college-major-search.

2. Search for a major that looks interesting to you.

3. Compare the major description with your Profile of Self, then complete a template below.

4. Complete three templates in total, one for each major.

**Major 1:** _____

What about this major most excites you?

_____

_____

_____

_____

_____

What about this major raises red flags or gives you pause and makes you think this might not be right for you?

_____

_____

_____

_____

_____

What questions do you have that might be useful to ask someone working in that field?

_____

_____

_____

_____

_____

Following the Profile of Self:

What <u>values</u> of the major seem aligned to your profile, both implicit and explicit? In other words, what values do you see in the description?

_____

_____

_____

_____

_____

What <u>talents</u> seem aligned? In other words, what talents pop up in the description?

_____

_____

_____

_____

_____

What <u>environmental factors</u> seem aligned? To what types of work environments might this major lend itself?

_____

_____

_____

_____

What percentage match would you say this major is to your authentic self?

_____

_____

_____

_____

Based on what you researched, how likely are you to declare this major, on a scale from 1-10 (1=Not likely, 10=Highly)? Why?

(Circle one)      1     2     3     4     5     6     7     8     9     10

_____

_____

_____

_____

_____

**Major 2:** _____

What about this major most excites you?

_____

_____

_____

_____

_____

What about this major raises red flags or gives you pause and makes you think this might not be right for you?

_____

_____

_____

_____

_____

What questions do you have that might be useful to ask someone working in that field?

_____

_____

_____

_____

_____

Following the Profile of Self:

What <u>values</u> of the major seem aligned to your profile, both implicit and explicit? In other words, what values do you see in the description?

_____

_____

_____

_____

What <u>talents</u> seem aligned? In other words, what talents pop up in the description?

_____

_____

_____

_____

What <u>environmental factors</u> seem aligned? To what types of work environments might this major lend itself?

_____

_____

_____

_____

_____

What percentage match would you say this major is to your authentic self?

_____

_____

Based on what you researched, how likely are you to declare this major, on a scale from 1-10 (1=Not likely, 10=Highly)? Why?

(Circle one)     1     2     3     4     5     6     7     8     9     10

_____

_____

_____

_____

_____

**Major 3:** _____

What about this major most excites you?

_____

_____

_____

_____

_____

What about this major raises red flags or gives you pause and makes you think this might not be right for you?

_____

_____

_____

_____

_____

What questions do you have that might be useful to ask someone working in that field?

_____

_____

_____

_____

_____

Following the Profile of Self:

What <u>values</u> of the major seem aligned to your profile, both implicit and explicit? In other words, what values do you see in the description?

_____

_____

_____

_____

_____

What <u>talents</u> seem aligned? In other words, what talents pop up in the description?

_____

_____

_____

_____

_____

What <u>environmental factors</u> seem aligned? To what types of work environments might this major lend itself?

_____

_____

_____

_____

_____

What percentage match would you say this major is to your authentic self?

_____

_____

Based on what you researched, how likely are you to declare this major, on a scale from 1-10 (1=Not likely, 10=Highly)? Why?

(Circle one)    1    2    3    4    5    6    7    8    9    10

_____

_____

_____

_____

**Final Exploration Reflection**

**Instructions:** Answer the questions below. Remember, you aren't locked into a choice yet. This is still part of exploration and represents only one of the twin engines.

What three majors look most interesting based on the research you conducted?

_____

_____

_____

_____

_____

What other majors might you explore?

_____

_____

_____

_____

_____

# Chapter 9

## Step Three - Connect

A few years back, I had a good friend in his mid-thirties who was considering a total career RESET. He had worked in a variety of industries from education to sales and now, based on his self-reflection and Profile of Self, he had decided to go to medical school and become a doctor...at 35...with a wife and four kids. Needless to say, when he came to me for advice, he tested even my passion and drive for pursuing one's purpose!

I asked him several questions to get a feel for how the career aligned with his Profile, and I could see the connections he was making. It made sense. But I wanted him to take one last step before diving headlong into six-figure debt to pursue this dream.

I challenged him to connect with a doctor at church (we had many in our congregation at the time because of our proximity to the medical center) and shadow them for a day. He agreed and found an emergency doctor who invited him to come and observe for an afternoon and see a variety of specialties at work.

Later that afternoon, I got a call from my friend on his way back from an afternoon of observation. I couldn't wait to hear his report, fully expecting him to tell me that he was head over heels in love with medicine.

"How was it?" I asked excitedly.

"It was great," he said. "I learned two things. One, I have no desire to be a doctor. That was horrible, man. It's just not for me. Two, you saved me $300,000 in student loan debt. Thank you!"

And just like that, he moved on to the next dream.

As a quick epilogue, I'm happy to report that he's living an outstanding life in California doing something he's great at — sales — and getting compensated to match his passion.

This is the power of connecting. It's not enough to simply read about a career. You have to go see it in action. You have to connect with the people doing the work that interests you to see what it's really like. You can only learn so much by researching a major or career online. But you can determine pretty rapidly whether something is a fit from a 30-minute conversation or an hour of shadowing.

**How I got on the path to my best-fit career**

When I was trying to figure out what to do with my life after the public relations debacle, I made a habit of informally interviewing every person I came across to figure out what they did for a living, why they chose that, and how they got there. This was a fascinating exercise. I learned two things:

1. Almost no one chose their career from the inside out.
2. Most people are more unhappy in their careers than you'd ever imagine.

In fact, many of the people I'd interview would turn the questions back on me: "So, what are you doing? And how are you figuring it out?"

However, in the course of interviewing people, I made a connection that changed my whole trajectory. I was talking with a good friend of mine who was a senior in college at the time at the University of Utah. I asked him what he was going to do when he graduated, and he said, "I may go into Student Affairs." I asked him what that was, and he said, "You know those people in college that work in the advising office, or the career office, or who run programs like orientation or outdoor recreation? Turns out those people get *paid* to do that."

No kidding. I had never imagined that. I figured they were faculty who did it as part of their service to the university.

He then made me an offer: "Check it out online, and if it looks interesting, I'm happy to connect you with Barb Snyder, the VP of Student Affairs at the University of Utah."

That afternoon, I researched it and felt that same feeling I'm asking you to look for — that motivating, warm, light, exciting feeling in your gut that says, "This is it."

I took him up on his offer and set up an interview with Barb. I dressed the part, met her in her office, and talked for the next 30 minutes about her career: why she chose it, how she spent her time each day, and how she got there. It was thrilling. She described mentoring students, teaching classes, running programs, and having a balanced life. She made a good salary, loved the energy of a university campus, and had lots of opportunities for professional development and growth. I was sold.

She recommended a handful of universities who were the best in the nation for Student Affairs and offered to be a resource for me throughout the process. I applied, got accepted to three of the five, and ultimately ended up at Indiana University.

That one small connection with my buddy altered my entire path. That's what connecting is all about. In this step, the goal is to do two things:

1. Take a job, career, or major you are considering and do no less than a few hours of on-site observation and shadowing.
2. Conduct informal and formal informational interviews with as many people as you can in the industry to learn more about the career.

Through these two actions, you'll have a crystal-clear understanding of what you're getting yourself into before you ever start. In fact, this combined with self-reflection and exploration will dramatically clarify your next step.

And it all starts with building your constellation.

## The Power of the Constellation

I often tell people the most important person you'll ever meet…is every person you meet.

I can trace virtually all of the 400+ people I've coached in the past few years and 150+ organizational clients back to approximately ten people.

Like the Kevin Bacon game, the degrees of separation are small between the clients who have supported my business and allowed me to continue to grow and a core group of friends and past colleagues. These were early followers, believers, supporters, and advocates.

Here's the catch: I didn't build a relationship with any of the "core ten" expecting to tap that relationship for future opportunity.

I built a relationship with them because I cared, I liked them, and I wanted to add whatever value I could.

Every interaction is an opportunity for connection and trust. And when you add value to other peoples' lives with no expectation of return, the law of reciprocity kicks in and balance is restored in the universe.

A simple contact today could mean a huge opportunity in the future.

Interestingly, this is the step where I sometimes lose people. Reflection is hard, and yet it's significantly less risky than this step, so most people have no problem doing it. But connecting is where it's at! This is it. This is where you catalyze opportunity for yourself, get significant clarity, and let the world know you exist. Don't bail on me. Hang in there and be intentional with this step.

<u>Build Your Constellation</u>

It's time to start building your constellation. What's that? Very simply, it's a visual map of all the connections you have in your entire life who may have some value to add in matching you to something you would love to do. I recommend mapping it in three stages. Go ahead and open a notebook now, create three columns, and label them Tier 1, Tier 2, and Tier 3. Aim for three to five people per tier. You may simply bullet point them with their name, title, and organization.

First, identify those people you are directly connected with who have a vested interest in your success and with whom you have some level of influence on account of the principles discussed above. They already buy into you. They may include parents, pastors, youth leaders, former employers, colleagues, former professors, career advisors, mentors, and close friends. List them in Tier 1 with their name, title, and organization.

Tier 1

_____

_____

_____

_____

_____

_____

_____

Next, identify those individuals who are one level further. These people may be familiar with you, but you may lack the influence to ask favors from them. Would you invite them to your wedding reception? Maybe. Would you ask them if you could borrow $20 for gas money? Not likely. These are family friends, former colleagues with whom you had a limited relationship, professors who know you but know nothing about you, cousins and extended family, next-level contacts on LinkedIn, that one guy from church that seems to have a cool job but with whom you've never talked about anything meaningful, and that guy in the lunchroom from your fantasy football league. These are Tier 2 contacts.

Tier 2

_____

_____

_____

_____

_____

_____

Now identify those people who have no interest in you but in whom you are interested. These might be people who you look at and think, "That's my job." They may be interesting professors, personalities, distant contacts on LinkedIn, or authors. List them in Tier 3.

Tier 3

_____

_____

_____

_____

_____

_____

_____

_____

Congrats! You've created a constellation of contacts, a veritable network you never knew you had.

<u>Make Connections</u>

The next step is to begin to connect. Your goal is to expand your horizons. You want to learn about as many jobs as possible to begin to sort through what might provide an opportunity for you to maximize your Profile of Self.

In any leadership program I develop, I build in a component called "executive interviews." The concept is simple: each participant is required to identify three people at the highest levels of an organization other than their own and interview them. These interviews serve several purposes:

1.  Build confidence. People are often intimidated by leaders in executive roles — that is, until they interview them. Turns out, leaders are just as human as the rest of us, and interviewing someone at a high level in an organization can build your confidence.

2.  Create connections. Perhaps the greatest outcome of these conversations is a new connection. Inevitably, as you interview these individuals, they end the session by asking the ultimate question: "Tell me about you. What do you want to do?"

3. Clarify pathways. How do you get where you want to go? I'm not sure. But I'll tell you who is — someone who is there. It's important to remember that their pathway may not work for you, but learning about the myriad pathways to the career you're after will spark ideas to catalyze action.

4. Break down unhelpful mindsets. *I can't do that. There's no one like me in that field. I don't fit the mold. I don't have the background.* All these statements, of course, are excuses and fixed mindsets that prevent us from moving forward. Nothing breaks these down like meeting and interviewing someone who wasn't the standard candidate but who scored the gig anyway.

Your goal, then, should be to do the same. Identify at least three individuals in industries or roles that interest you and interview them. Learn about who they are, how they ended up in their position, and what advice they might have for you. I'd recommend connecting with at least one person from each Tier.

What you ask is important. I recommend the four "golden" questions:

- What do you do?
- What does that mean?
- Why do you do it?
- How did you get there?

You might also try some of these:

Values

- Why did you choose this career?
- Why do people stay? Why do people leave?
- What about this field most lights your fire?
- What do people love most about this organization?
- Thinking about leaders who you've seen be successful, what drives them?

Talents

- What do you do every day?
- What does a typical day look like?
- What about the job energizes you?
- What skills do the most successful people possess?
- What skill sets are most valuable in this role?
- What sets apart a strong leader from an average one?

Environments

- What do people like about the environment here? How would you describe it?
- How would you describe the culture in the office? The vibe?
- What is your office environment like?
- How much interaction do you have with others?
- Do you travel?
- How do people stay balanced?
- What does autonomy look like in this role?

As you listen to the answers, look for your **values, talents, and environments** to emerge. Does it seem to align? As they describe their work, do you feel energized? Excited?

You may not get a chance to ask all of these questions but pick one to two in each category and take good notes to get a comprehensive view of the three things that make up organizations. You might also ask some of the "red flag" questions from the reflective activity. Then compare them with your Profile of Self to listen for "Is this a fit?"

Most importantly, when the law of reciprocity kicks in, be ready. Inevitably they will say, "So, what are you interested in?" Or they might ask, "What are you looking for?" Don't overwhelm them, but share some of the statements from your Profile of Self. This might sound like, "I'm not sure what it's called in the workforce, but I want to use my knack for connecting with people, strategizing, creating structure, and starting programs. I love autonomy in my work and being around lots of people in a fast-paced environment." Then, turn it back on them: "Does this sound like what you do? Or have you heard of jobs like this along your journey?" Don't make a direct ask unless they offer. Your goal is to learn. That's it. But this contact could yield an internship or job one day, so make the connection.

These interviews are not as difficult to secure as it may seem. People are generally very willing to talk with a career-seeker. The keys are sincerity and respect for their schedule. Keep the interviews to no more than 30 minutes unless they suggest otherwise. It's always better to land one of these interviews through a warm connection such as a friend or colleague who can introduce you. That said, if cold calling is your only option to make the connection, follow these rules:

- Demonstrate that you know something about the organization

- In your cold email, drop a name of someone you both know or something you have in common (e.g., a college advisor or mentor, teacher or professor, both alumni of the same college, both lived in the same place for a time, etc.)

- Be clear about your ask and flexible with scheduling, suggesting many options that may work

The ultimate goal is to simply be intentional. Become a learner. Sit down with people you are interested in, you admire, or who are several more steps down the career path and learn from them. Opportunities arise from human connections, and those connections are forged one authentic conversation at a time.

Finally, you may choose to use something like the email template below to initiate the conversation:

Hi _____,

My name is _____ and [insert common connection here]. (You may also follow-up with a sentence here such as "I've really enjoyed your book and learned..." or "I'm a junior at X college exploring various careers..." or "I'm trying to get a feel for other roles in the profession.")

I'd love to connect for 30 minutes in the coming weeks to learn more about what you do. Would you be available for a phone call or to meet up on either [insert at least two dates with at least two available options for times]? I'm open to other times as well.

I look forward to connecting!

Sincerely,

Your Name

By the way, what should you do after? Show *gratitude*! Send them a note, tell them something they said that resonated, and thank them for their time. If appropriate, attach a copy of your Profile of Self to show them more about who you are (but only if they express interest). If you really know them well, you might attach a resume and ask them to keep an eye out for jobs or internships that look like they might be a fit. No pressure, but if they see something, they could let you know.

Voila! An army of ambassadors will start looking for your best-fit work *on your behalf.* By the way, how many of these conversations should you have before you start to narrow down a college major? The magic number is *five*, which amounts to 1-2 people from each tier. I don't know why, but when people have less than five conversations, they simply don't get the information or momentum they need to make a decision. Having more than five conversations is excellent, so don't let me limit you. But talk to *at least* five people from across your tiers and watch the momentum work!

With self-reflection, exploration, and connection in full swing, it's almost time to narrow down your decision. What's interesting to me is that most of us go from trying to choose a major to deciding an option without ever doing Steps One, Two, and Three. Think of all you would have missed out on by not applying the pages of content between where we started and where we are now. Before we decide, we first need to consider the role of money. It is, after all, one of the top extrinsic motivators. Also, we need it to live. We'll then take a look at a few methods for making hard decisions, with the aim of helping you narrow down your options in the next few pages.

**TAKE ACTION:** So now you know who you are and have an idea what type of work would energize you! However, all of the self-reflection, reading, and researching in the world can't take the place of **connecting with actual human beings** and getting **hands-on experience** with your top career choices.

**Instructions:** Your goal is to connect with *at least* three people to start, ideally one from each career of interest. After completing each conversation, fill out a template below to capture your key learnings and other important information. But remember: the magic number is five or more. Don't stop short!

### 1. Informational Interviews

**Connection #1 Name:**

_____

How do you know this person?

_____

_____

_____

_____

What did you learn about their profession that was most intriguing?

_____

_____

_____

_____

Following the Profile of Self:

What <u>values</u> did they describe about their career that seem aligned to your profile, both implicit and explicit?

_____

_____

_____

_____

_____

What <u>talents</u> seem aligned?

_____

_____

_____

_____

What <u>environmental factors</u> seem aligned? What type of work environment might someone in this career be in?

_____

_____

_____

_____

What percentage match would you say this career is to your authentic self?

_____

_____

What path did they follow to get where they are?

_____

_____

_____

_____

**Connection #2 Name:**

_____

How do you know this person?

_____

_____

_____

_____

What did you learn about their profession that was most intriguing?

_____

_____

_____

_____

Following the Profile of Self:

What <u>values</u> did they describe about their career that seem aligned to your profile, both implicit and explicit?

_____

_____

_____

_____

_____

What <u>talents</u> seem aligned?

_____

_____

_____

_____

What <u>environmental factors</u> seem aligned? What type of work environment might someone in this career be in?

_____

_____

_____

_____

What percentage match would you say this career is to your authentic self?

_____

_____

What path did they follow to get where they are?

_____

_____

_____

_____

**Connection #3 Name:**

_____

How do you know this person?

_____

_____

_____

_____

_____

What did you learn about their profession that was most intriguing?

_____

_____

_____

_____

_____

Following the Profile of Self:

What <u>values</u> did they describe about their career that seem aligned to your profile, both implicit and explicit?

_____

_____

_____

_____

_____

What <u>talents</u> seem aligned?

_____

_____

_____

_____

What <u>environmental factors</u> seem aligned? What type of work environment might someone in this career be in?

_____

_____

_____

_____

What percentage match would you say this career is to your authentic self?

_____

_____

What path did they follow to get where they are?

_____

_____

_____

_____

_____

## 2. Hands-on Experience

In addition to informational interviews, taking advantage of hands-on experience is the best way to get invaluable insights regarding your best-fit career. I encourage you to be **strategic** and proactive about participating in extracurricular activities related to your areas of interest. Below is a quick list of ideas for gaining hands-on experience.

1. **Summer enrichment programs** are often offered by local colleges or non-profit organizations. They have a predetermined curriculum to teach students about the content matter at hand and provide opportunities for creating related projects. Some enrichment programs include field trips or inviting professional guest speakers. Programs range from a few days to a few weeks and can be free or up to a couple thousand dollars. You can find these programs by simply typing "summer enrichment program + location + career

field" into a Google search bar. Your school counselors may also have some informational pamphlets to share.

2. **Internships** are on-site job experiences. Students will work at the site or office building of a professional in that industry. Some internships involve doing basic administrative tasks while others provide opportunities to participate in content-related projects and meetings. Be sure to ask the host company what your responsibilities would be during the internship so you can get a feel for how useful the experience will be.

3. **Shadowing a professional** — If you cannot find a program or internship to attend, you can reach out to an industry professional to see if they would be willing to let you shadow them for a day of work. This is a great way to get a feel for what the work environment is like and what are the day-to-day tasks of this job.

4. **Clubs and organizations** — Be sure to use high school extracurricular activities as an opportunity to explore your field of interest. Many clubs work on content-related projects during the year, and some may bring in guest speakers or go on relevant field trips. If your school doesn't have a club or organization related to the career or major you are interested in, consider starting the first chapter!

5. **Meetup.com** is a great place to meet people and attend events related to your interests. You can join groups that interest you and will receive notifications when they are hosting events in your area. Warning: Most meetups are for adults, so alcohol is sometimes provided, and *anyone* can host a meet-up, so it's not always put on by a reputable company.

6. **Community college courses** — Most community colleges will allow you to register for an introductory course in any subject. You can take these classes during the summer or on a night or weekend during the school year. This is a great way to get a feel for what majoring in a certain subject may be like.

7. **University weekend informationals** — Most universities have weekend events for prospective students and families. Some are for the general university, while others are specific to individual colleges within the university (i.e., School of Business). These events may be a one-day event or an overnight event where prospective students can spend a night in a college dorm and shadow a current student. These are extremely useful experiences in helping high school students decide where they want to go to college and what they may want to major in. Check university websites and use Google to search for these types of opportunities.

**Final Connect Reflection**

**Instructions:** Answer the question below.

Based on everything I've researched and the people I've connected with, what is my first-choice major? Why?

_____

_____

_____

_____

_____

# Chapter 10

## Weigh the Role of Money

A few years ago, I read this anecdote from *True North* by Bill George:

Citing a recent visit with business school students, Dave Cox, former CEO of Cowles Media, quoted one as saying, "Maybe I have to get my satisfaction someplace else and I'll just do the business part to make money." Amazed by the comment, Cox raised his eyebrows quizzically, "Why would you want to spend your time doing work you don't enjoy? These should be the best years of your life. There is so much energy that results from feeling valued and connecting with what you're enthusiastic about. That is when you add the greatest value."

I love that he was amazed by the comment, as in, "What on earth is this person thinking? Just making money to one day enjoy it?"

I, for one, am not amazed. I've seen it quite literally a thousand times over the past 20 years. In fact, almost every person I coach today is someone who didn't have a chance to read this book and get it right when they were 22. And typically, the number one influencer of career is money.

Why?

Well, it turns out that we need it for everything. Food, shelter, transportation, healthcare, recreation, bacon. You name it. And yet, it should never be the primary driver of career.

Why not? I'm glad you asked.

First, why do people stay in jobs? Interestingly, money is a main reason why people take jobs, but it doesn't even crack the top ten reasons people stay. According to one study, people stay in their jobs for these 10 reasons:

1. Career growth, learning, and development
2. Exciting work and challenge
3. Meaningful work, making a difference
4. Great people
5. Being part of a team
6. Recognition
7. Fun on the job
8. Autonomy, sense of control over my work
9. Flexibility — work hours, dress code
10. Inspiring leadership

(From a 2015 survey by Jordan, Evans, and Kay of 2,200 respondents across 20 industries, in order of frequency.)

Where's money? Not on that list. Because once you get the job and the money starts rolling in, you don't think about it often. Rather, your day-to-day satisfaction is mostly determined by the top ten above.

This is all the more reason why the money/happiness theory makes sense.

I developed this theory almost 20 years ago when I was making $39k a year working for a university. Back then it was just a theory...a hypothesis. But I set out to prove it as more than a theory — a reality. And sure enough, it's become true for me and hundreds of my clients.

The theory says this:

When people choose money over happiness, those two factors operate on opposing continuums, with money increasing rapidly and happiness declining. The more money you make, the less happy you become as you get paid, promoted, and rewarded to do less and less of the things you enjoy...the very things you sacrificed when you chose money over happiness in the first place. We call this the "golden handcuffs," which means you get paid so well that you can't afford to leave. I've coached people who make $250k, $500k, and even a million dollars a year and who hate it. It's hard to understand, I know. But it's a true phenomenon.

On the other hand, when you choose happiness over money, they both operate on parallel upward trajectories. Sure, you may make less money to begin with, but you won't stay there long. And your money will never decrease for doing what you love. In fact, as you do things that make you happy, your money will increase and, over time, you'll get paid, promoted, and rewarded to do the things you loved to do anyway.

M = Money
H = Happiness Quotient

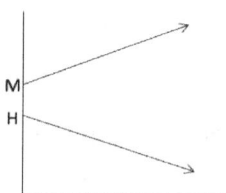
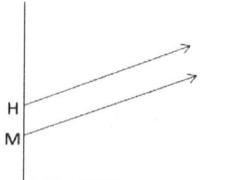

So, choose something that makes you happy first and foremost. As you look at the list of majors you're considering, which one seems most interesting? Which one makes you feel excited, motivated, inspired, or causes you to yearn to learn more? Choose that one. And guess what? If it doesn't fit, you'll know and can pivot to something else. Make the best decision you can with the information you have now. When you have more information, re-evaluate.

A while back, I went to a college fair where departments shared information for prospective students to help them make decisions about what to be involved in. I floated over to the Dance and Theater department to talk with the representative from the dance major. My daughter is a gifted dancer, and I was curious what background most people bring to the program.

This guy spoke my language. As we got to talking, he said that he had chosen to be a dance major in college many years ago because he felt drawn to it, it interested him, and he got energy from doing it. He hadn't danced much before then but wanted to learn about it. When he told his friends and family he was going to major in dance, they were floored. I'm sure he heard many of the things most people say when someone else's path doesn't fit with their own expectations for that person. Why that? You can't make money in that. What will you do to balance that out?

Nevertheless, he pursued it with vigor and graduated. After college, he developed his own niche of interest in dance, and became so good at it that people sought him out for his skills. He was hired as faculty and now runs the Dance department, while making money on the side as a private tutor and expert. I applauded him for pursuing his passion, and he said, "When you choose something you love, the universe has a way of shifting to make it possible for you to do that thing, no matter how uncharted the path." I couldn't agree more. Like Robert Frost's epic poem says, the road less traveled makes all the difference.

## Money Myths

By the way, why is it so difficult to choose happiness over money? Generally, when I teach this to college students, I hear three common arguments. Allow me to share those now with a few thoughts and anecdotes to debunk each of them.

1. "You can't make money doing that."

*Translation: Are you sure anybody makes actual money in that job? Seems more like a hobby to me. Anyway, even if somebody is making money at it, I probably wouldn't.*

I met with a woman the other day whose husband just retired from a job he hated for most of his career. I was shocked.

"Why did he do it?"

She said he had graduated in architecture, but after a year of doing it decided, "You can't make money in architecture" and jumped to a job that paid more but had horrible quality of life.

Again, I was shocked. I don't know much about architecture, but I know enough to know that someone is making money in architecture or else we would have no architects.

I spoke with a friend the other day who was facing the same dilemma. He's a born educator with a passion for marriage counseling. He's felt drawn back to that career path over and over by his inner voice, but each time he starts down the path, the thought surfaces, "You can't make money doing that..." and it's enough to dissuade him.

Meanwhile, the world is in need of passionate, talented marriage counselors more than ever.

Now it may be a reality that most people don't make a lot of money in the career you're considering. But the reality is that there's a range of salaries in every field. In fact, 15.8% of people in that field are making great money in that. Exceptional money.

But it's likely true that the rest aren't, because career operates on a bell curve, like most anything else in life.

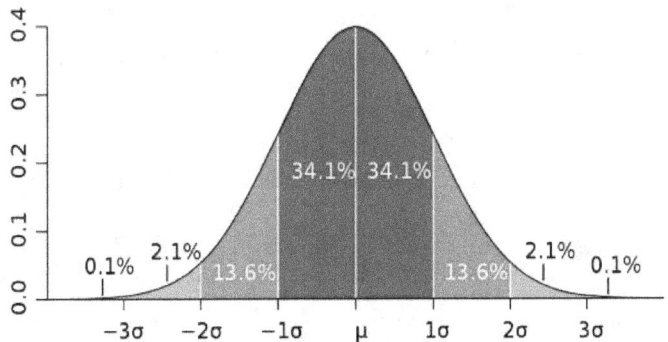

- The bottom 15.8% make bad money. Like, terrible.
- The middle 68.2% make good money, equal to their skill set — "good."
- The top 15.8%? Exceptional money.

So, if the majority of the industry you're interested in doesn't make good money, should that stop you?

The short answer is generally "no."

Since when do you pursue your passion to become part of the ~85% that doesn't make money?

The X factor is time — how long until you become one of the top earners in that industry. I can't answer that for your specific situation, but I can tell you that those who are at the top all have at least one thing in common — they love the work and are good at it. They get clear about their strengths and contribute them as often as possible to add value to the world around them. And they stick with it through the ups and downs.

There are probably lots of other things that set them apart, but the truth is that people who love what they do rise to the top and get paid. And people who love what they do are people who choose something they love and do what they do best to add value to it.

Plain and simple.

When I started my career, I wanted to teach seminary for my church, but the naysaying voices were overwhelming. *"You can't earn enough money doing that. How will you support a family? What will your day job be? You just spent tens of thousands of dollars on a Public Relations degree, what about that?"* In fact, in one of the early classes I took, the professor said that only a handful out of the whole crowd would ever make it as professional seminary teachers. He confirmed what I was already thinking. I couldn't do it. So, I bailed on it and only came back to it six years later. Turns out you can make money in it. In fact, the best can make a great living doing it. However, I didn't know that at the time. I just accepted that it wouldn't work out for me.

If we're going to use this excuse, we should at least say, "I don't believe *I* can make money doing that" instead of "*you* can't make any money doing that." Let's call this out for what it really is. It is a limiting belief that is founded on the idea that you couldn't possibly be good enough. But if you have arrived at this career choice because it is rooted in your values, talents, and environments, you likely are good enough. Maybe you could become one of the best if you're willing to put in the time and effort to develop the career.

So don't let "You can't make money in that!" hold you back. Someone's making money in that. Really good money. Might as well be you.

2. "What if what I love doesn't pay?"

*Translation: What I love doesn't pay **me** right now. Maybe it would eventually, but I'm not willing to wait that long. There are a thousand steps/obstacles between me and a real income.*

Several weeks ago, I guest-lectured for a college career class about how to figure out what to do with your life. I hit 'em with the best stuff I have — beware the outside/in model, develop your Profile of Self, and fight the fears that get in the way of success.

Toward the end, a student who had a particularly skeptical look on her face and who had been fighting some internal voice during the whole session finally raised her hand.

"But what if what I love to do doesn't pay?"

Great question. I'm so glad she asked, because I guarantee each of you have thought this at least once, as has every other career-searcher in the world.

I returned volley with this: "Who's the best florist on planet earth?"

Any idea? Me neither. Until I looked it up. Google it. Some guy named Gregor, who is the Master of all Master Florists — essentially the Picasso of flowers. This guy has won awards for flowers internationally, has written 30 books, and speaks six languages.

And I guarantee he's not making $30k a year.

A florist, for heaven's sake. Killing it in the world of flowers.

Here's the best part: you can do this with any industry. Trash collectors, plumbers, artists, writers, mechanics, etc. Someone has to be the best. Every industry has someone at the top.

And what makes them the best at what they do is that they love it. There is always room at the top for those who love what they do.

It started with passion. It started with a drive to do it because they were intrinsically motivated by the craft, whatever that was.

So don't give me this "what if it doesn't pay" thing. Start with passion, add in some consistent hard work, earned credibility, networking, education and training, and do it all over a consistent period of time, and you will make money doing it.

3. "I can't make *enough* money doing that."

*Translation: This job will not immediately, or maybe ever, support the living I want. It would be easier to just pick a higher paying job right now. … Hmm? What's my budget? Well, I've never really done one, but I can just tell that I'll need more money. Besides, there's plenty of time for a gratifying career when I retire, right?*

So how much money is *enough*? Remember earlier when I mentioned that humans are really bad at estimating? Holds true in this case too.

The issue I want to address here is that people are not always clear about the financial component of getting from where they are to where they want to be. They just make the unquestioned assumption that their desired career will not yield enough money. But again, what is enough?

I posed the question during a budgeting lesson recently in a youth Sunday School class: "How much money do you think you want to make?" One kid said $15 an hour with large, greedy eyes. Another said, "Hm, $44 million dollars?"

Mid-career clients experience this disconnect too. I'll ask, "How much do you need to support yourself?" They'll look at me confused and generally have only a vague idea. Occasionally, they'll offer up some random number that is unrealistically high like the single mom I coached who has one daughter at home and said, "Well, I can't see myself getting by on any less than $150,000." Now I try to withhold judgment, because everyone's lifestyle is different, but I'm also a firm believer that we can generally live happily on less than we think.

Thankfully, there's a better way to approach this than estimating. Make a budget for yourself where you identify how much you need. Once your salary reaches that number, no amount of money beyond that number will have a significant impact on your happiness. You can then be sure that any unhappiness or dissatisfaction in life is simply a matter of misplaced priorities and values incongruence and not a genuine need to have more.

When a client says, "I can't make enough money at that," it tells me that they're not truly clear on either how much the salary for a career actually is or that they're unclear on how much money they actually need.

## The Survive and Thrive Budgets

I always advise my clients to create a "Survive and Thrive" budget (download the template at dustinpeterson.org/findyourfit). This is simply a two-column budget. The left side is what it would take to survive. This number should be really low. Like, uncomfortably low. That's why it's called a "survive" budget. The goal is simple: identify the minimum amount you need to keep a roof over your head, lights on, food on the table, gas in the car, and clothes on backs. Period. This is your financial floor, the number below which you cannot sustain life. I've had clients come back with their Survive budgets completed and "eating out" listed as a budget item. Wrong. We're talking basics.

Now create a Thrive budget on the right side. How much do you need to be truly happy? Dream a little bit. If you have a significant other, do this with them. What kind of life do you want to live when you've "made it?" How much will you set aside for vacation, car, and retirement? How much eating out will you do? Be generous, but not excessive, then total the number at the bottom. You now have your ceiling, or the number after which each additional dollar will not bring its equivalent in happiness. Will this number change in the future? Sure. But for now, it gives you a range that makes sense given your present circumstances — from Survive to Thrive — and you can more realistically plan your next step. The salary for the job you're applying for should fit nicely in that range, and ideally closer to the right.

Don't skip this step. I promise you, money and fear will continue to cause resistance. You'll work through the entire book only to say, "But I don't think I can afford to work in that major or career path." That would tell me that you didn't get clear about your numbers.

### Final Note on Money

I led a five-session Mastermind group recently with a group of people looking to RESET their careers, and one of the five sessions was entirely on money. That's how important it is. You can't ignore it.

As I said at the beginning of this chapter, we need money to live. It will certainly factor into your decision-making process. But don't forget where it ranks. Money makes a great follower and never a great leader. Let it be a piece of your decision, but don't let it lead.

Remember, fit always comes first.

# Chapter 11

## Decide

So, the moment of decision has come. You've researched myriad options and begun to circle around the same few. They all feel good in certain ways. But *how* do you decide?

Let me share with you a few of the approaches that have most helped me (and others) make tough decisions.

Before I do, and in the spirit of not burying the lead, let me give you the clearest answer:

**Choose fit.**

That's it. Choose the one that best seems to align with who you are. As we discussed at the beginning of the book, don't put anything in the first decision-making position except fit.

That said, if the decision isn't immediately clear, there are a couple of other strategies you can use to guide your decision-making process.

**Flip A Coin**

Stick with me here. This method is more reflective than it sounds.

Big decisions can be gut-wrenching. In the past 18 years, I have moved a family of six seven times, and I have worked seven jobs in a variety of industries. None of those decisions came easily. However, in making each decision, I used a consistent formula. This formula was given to me by a mentor in my graduate school days and has worked time and time again.

As with most methods geared toward self-improvement, don't be fooled by the simplicity of it. This takes some work, and you have to stick to it. If you do, I think you will find an increase in clarity as you work through the questions at hand. So, here's the strategy:

When choosing between two options, try them both on for a day and see how they feel.

David Brooks, the New York Times columnist, said it best at a commencement speech at Rice University. For all decisions aside from marriage, flip a coin. "But don't go by how the coin flips," he said. "Go by your emotional reaction to the coin flip. Are you happy or sad it came up heads or tails? That is your deepest self telling you what it wants."

Pure genius. And it works. When I was in graduate school and nearing the completion of my master's degree, I began contemplating the decision to either stay on and push toward a Ph.D. or go into the world of work and continue to figure out my life.

I sat with my mentor and asked him what he thought I should do. He told me to pick a day, any day, and make it the day that I decided to go on for a Ph.D. Tell people what you decided and live as if that was what you were going to do. Then, throughout the day, or at the very least at the end of the day, write down how you feel. Did you find yourself questioning it? Justifying it? Did you feel a sense of dread in your stomach or a rush of energy? Were you excited to tell people, or did you only share on a need-to-know basis? Then do the same thing with the other side of the coin. I did this, and it was clear as day that I should move into the workforce. As I shared my Ph.D. ambitions, I felt inauthentic and empty. But when I talked about getting a job, I lit up, and my general countenance shined.

Others were able to tell me what I already knew deep down: I had already made the decision, but I needed to figure it out for myself.

Try the same with a college major you're looking at. Recently, my wife and I took our daughter on a college tour. It was fun and fascinating to see how she responded to people who asked, "So what major are you considering?" Over the course of the weekend, as she learned more about the myriad options in the world, she went from English Education to Digital Media Marketing and even Dance and Theater. Where she ultimately ends up is still to be determined, but I noticed a visible shift in her energy when she talked about and "claimed" one major over another. One option felt and sounded more subdued, more duty-bound, and more practical, while she described others in an animated, even authentic tone. I'll leave out which is which since she'll likely read this book and the decision is ultimately hers, but the anecdote holds power.

Pick a major and when people ask that ever-annoying question, "What are you going to study," try it on for size. How does it feel to say it? When others ask you to tell them why or explain more, does it come easily? Naturally? Do you feel excited and strong? Or do you feel like you're giving up, doing the "practical" thing, and justifying that major?

As I mentioned before, with most people, I believe you intuitively already have a strong feel for what you would like to pursue. We just have to silence the extrinsic pressures long enough to align the inner and outer self.

By the way, a byproduct of using this method is solid confirmation that this is the path to take — you can reflect on the feelings you had and the notes you took that were evidence to you that this is what you should do. This is increasingly important as the dark clouds form to cast doubt on your mind the closer you draw to "the day" to follow the decision.

## Find Convergence

A while back, my good friend sent me an image that described your purpose in life as the convergence of four things:

1. What you love.
2. What you're good at.
3. What you can be paid for.
4. What the world needs.

Use these to screen your potential college major choice! Not all majors are created equal, and some may prepare you for two or three but not all four. For example, you may love basket-weaving (1) and be really good at it (2), but not make any money doing it (3) nor does the world really need it (4). On the other hand, you might major in accounting because the world needs it (4) and you can be paid for it (3) and you might even be good at it (2) but totally hate it (1). Don't do it. If you need a reason why, go back and read this whole book.

Of course, be careful here. Remember Gregor, the florist. There is always room at the top of any industry for those who love what they do. Someone has to be the Department Chair in Basket Weaving and get paid to do it. Someone else is the top accountant, the expert ice-cream store manager, the super competent and highly compensated pipe layer, or the unrivaled painter or musician. If you love it, you'll rise.

**TAKE ACTION:** Reflect on your decision-making process. It is likely that you've surfaced several options that would fit your unique set of values, talents, and environments. If you've done the work of identifying options that fit, there's not a wrong choice.

1. In previous chapters, you were asked to identify the percentage fit of each major or job. Which option had the highest percentage fit?

_____

_____

_____

2. How did it feel to flip the coin or try on each decision for a day? Which option(s) felt the most natural and exciting? Which option(s), if any, felt duty-bound or like you were settling?

_____

_____

_____

_____

3. Which option had the most compelling convergence of factors (what you love, what you're good at, what you can be paid for, what the world needs)?

_____

_____

_____

_____

4. Is there one option that you're drawn to more than the others? What draws you to that major?

_____

_____

_____

_____

_____

5. Which option sparks your curiosity the most? Which one has the most interesting internship and volunteer opportunities?

_____

_____

_____

_____

_____

6. Are you feeling any strong hesitations about any of your choices? What are they? Are they genuine safety or solvency concerns? Or are they rooted in fear as discussed in Chapter 5?

_____

_____

_____

_____

_____

# Chapter 12

## Start Walking the Path

I recently went to Moab, an amazing spot in Utah for hiking. On the first day, we drove to the parking lot for our first excursion, made a quick lunch, put on sunscreen, grabbed some water, and went to the trailhead to look at the map and decide which trail to take.

One trail would take us one direction, and another trail would take us the other. Both ended up at the same spot, but they each had potentially different vistas, terrain, and experiences.

Based on feedback from the park ranger, who had been down the trails before, and based on gut instinct, we picked one.

Did we pick the right one? Who knows. We'll likely never know. But we made the most of it regardless and enjoyed the journey.

Imagine for a second that we stood at the trailhead all day long, paralyzed to decide because we didn't know for sure that we would pick the right trail. The extent of my trip would have been a view of the trailhead and a whole lot of "what might have been."

Welcome to the world of 90% of career clients I coach.

"Which way is right?"

"What if I pick wrong?"

"How can I know for sure that it will work out?"

Behold — a few key lessons from the anecdote:

1.  The first step is to get to the right place. If your passion is X mountain (read: ARENA), then navigate to the mountain and pick a path. It doesn't so much matter which path but pick something. If, however, your passion is X mountain and you are on the prairies of the Midwest, then you're not even in the right playing field (again, read: ARENA). Figure out your passion, then pick a path. Passionate about the law? Get into a major that preps you for law, such as English, Psychology, Business, or Political Science/Policy. Like social movements? Try Non-Profit Management, Sociology, Education, or Social Work. Interested in math? Go Engineering, Math, or Finance. The key is to get in the right arena and go from there. If you've made it that far, there isn't really a wrong choice. You're likely stuck because you need some experience to inform your next decision, but don't pick law if you love math.

2.  Don't let preparation get in the way. Are there risks? Sure. Dehydration. Starvation. Sunburn. We did some prep to prevent those things from occurring but took no more time than was needed to prepare. Get to the trailhead. Preparation can be an excuse to never leave the car.

3.  Seek advice from those who've navigated the trails. Once you find your passion (X mountain), ask someone who's been down those paths. This is where everyone gets stuck. "I love animals, and think I want to be a vet, but don't know the next step." Then go interview a vet or two or three and learn from them. Love cooking? Interview a

chef. Flying? Interview a pilot. Talk to people who've done it. Their insight can tell you a lot about the paths you're considering.

If you're at the trailhead, you're in a good spot. It means you've done the research and reflection to figure out generally what you want to do with your life. Now don't get stuck trying to pick the right path. Again, there isn't a wrong decision at this point. You identified these options as being aligned with your unique profile. In other words, they're all good options for you.

Just choose from the options you identified. Remember, you identified these choices as being aligned with your unique profile. In other words, they're all good options for you. You can always turn back, jump trails, or carve a new path.

**What if I make the wrong decision?**

Wouldn't it be neat if we could predict the future? Turns out, most people can't do that. We know this, and yet we let fear of the unknown stop us from moving forward with decisions that we actually feel pretty strongly about. In other words, we get stuck at the trailhead.

A few years ago, I spoke at a conference in Florida and while I was there I met an interesting guy. We sat down for 30 minutes or so and explored his strengths and talents so that he could use this information to decide on a career path.

As we talked, it was obvious that he was crystal clear about his strengths. He was exceptional at things like "arranging materials to produce a product that benefits people." He had used this strength for years doing mock-ups of houses just for fun. He had shadowed a construction manager for a summer and loved the experience.

All signs pointed to him finding satisfaction in architecture or construction management.

So why did he need my help?

I asked him this in not so many words. I think my exact question was, "So why don't you do it?"

His answer: "I'm afraid to make the wrong decision. What if I choose it, invest in it, get down the road, and decide it's not for me?"

First, this is a totally understandable way to think. I've thought the same many times. But I've also learned through my own experience three important principles:

1.  There is no "right" career, as I mentioned at the beginning of this book. The truth is that you can work in any number of careers, industries, and organizations as long as they align with your talents, values, and ideal working environment. There isn't a right or wrong, but there is definitely a worst, better, and best, and the easiest way to narrow these down is through self-exploration. Start with what you do know — you.

2.  We all experience fear in some form or another as we move along our career paths. It is human nature, and you're not alone if you've felt it. But if you don't face the fear and move anyway, you're ensuring that you stay in the unsatisfying situation you were in before.

3. You can always reset. Use the process you learned in this book to help you. Inevitably, once you get started on your path toward a best-fit major or career, you'll find that your perceptions about the field you chose will change. That's what happens as you live the experience. Some parts may feel affirming, while others turn out not to be what you expected. At that point, you can re-evaluate. Reflect on the experiences you have and pivot.

That's why I exist — to help people reset. So, make a choice today knowing that you've got a parachute in the future to help bail you out if the work gets dicey. I'm here for you and will always provide free resources at dustinpeterson.org.

**A Note on Setbacks**

I would be remiss if I didn't address the possibility of setbacks. I promised you the truth, right? Just because you know who you are and make aligned choices does not mean you will be immune from failure, setbacks, and disappointments. But don't let that stop you from taking the next step! Remember, there are many paths and much to learn along the way. Don't let a little obstacle on the trail ruin your whole experience.

**Never Count Yourself Out**

I witnessed an interesting phenomenon when I was teaching at Rice University. At the time, I helped select and coordinate a small group of students who acted as an advisory board to our leadership department. They were tasked with providing us feedback, collaborating on programs, and being ambassadors for our initiatives. Historically, students had either been appointed or had expressed interest and had been selected. One year, we decided to change the process and we sent an email to all of our past students asking them to simply email us if they were interested and to include a brief explanation of what they felt they could add to the group.

We were surprised by the slim number of submissions. We had thought the advisory board was more of a draw, and yet almost nobody applied.

Several days later, after talking with a few students, we discovered that many highly capable and qualified students had decided not to apply at all because they looked at their peers who may also be applying and didn't feel they could compete. They turned themselves down for the program before ever applying!

I repeat…they turned themselves down.

Many of them may have been fantastic candidates. In addition, even if they weren't selected that year we may have been more likely to consider them next year. I was baffled. What could cause these outstanding students to self-select out of the program before ever even giving it a shot?! Why would they not simply send an email with a short statement of interest, just to see what happens?? Ironically, I knew exactly why. I could empathize, and this experience got me thinking about the many, many things that I've counted myself out of before ever giving them a chance. Here is a short list:

- I got cut in basketball tryouts in 10th grade. I came back stronger, taller (6'4"), and with better skills the following year, walked into the gym on the first day of tryouts, looked at my competition, and turned around and walked out, deciding it wasn't worth it to fail again.

- During my sophomore year in college, I made a name for myself around campus and felt I had hit my social peak. I had a talent for relating with others and was a good communicator. I also had some good ideas of ways to change the campus for the better. I was primed to run for student body president (even at the urging of others), but decided not to submit my name because I talked myself out of it, believing that maybe I didn't have that much value to add.

- As I was getting ready to graduate, I decided I wanted to pursue a career teaching seminary for my church full-time. Teaching is a natural talent and something that I find very rewarding. Although not high-paying, I felt that this would be a very fulfilling career. The process includes three semester-long courses, some in-class teaching evaluations, and a few interviews. On the first day of the first class, the trainer revealed some statistics stating that less than five people are generally selected to teach from a class of 32 prospects. I looked around the class, determined that there was no way I would make it, and backed out.

Now, I don't share these examples to elicit pity but rather to empathize. I know personally the feeling of allowing my fears to overwhelm my confidence and trump my strengths. Looking back, I believe I could have succeeded at any one of these three (and countless other) goals. And yet, before I ever got started I discounted my abilities and allowed my inner critic to talk me out of success.

I often tell my clients, "don't ever reject yourself. Always let someone else do it." The spirit of this advice is this: if you have an inkling to apply and throw your name in the hat, do it. You never know what may come of an opportunity. But what if you do it and get rejected? What if you aren't accepted into your program of choice, or you get rejected from that internship you had your heart set on? What if you fail a class you need to finish your program? In short, what if things don't work out how you had hoped?

As we discussed in the trail hiking story earlier, there is more than one way to reach your destination.

You *will* experience setbacks. You won't always get accepted, invited, promoted, or experience success. But career is a journey, not an event. Each experience will open the door to new reflection, discovery, and opportunity, so find another way.

## Setbacks Give you an Opportunity to Re-evaluate

While at Rice, we ran a competitive internship program. We always had around 100 applications for 30 spots, and those students who weren't accepted experienced some measure of loss, hopelessness, or despair. The week after we would send the acceptance and rejection letters, we'd have a flood of visitors in our office expressing disappointment. Some would ask for feedback. Very few would ever apply again.

I was most impressed by a student I worked with who applied two years in a row. Neither application was a good representation of who he was, and his interviews did not go well. He was extrinsically motivated and lacked introspection, and that showed in his application and interactions. Alas, he was never accepted into the program, but we formed a bond anyway. I was impressed with his resilience. I told him I'd personally mentor him and help him get where he wanted to go.

He ultimately graduated, found a job in oil and gas, and started his career at a highly successful company. Before long, he was unhappy. It wasn't a true fit. The rigor of the job and the misalignment with his Profile of Self catalyzed the exact introspection he lacked many years earlier when applying for the Rice internship program. Now he did the hard work of figuring out what he wanted from his career and what was important in his life, and he made a leap. He quit his job, traveled for a time, started a marketing company, explored his previously undeveloped passion for art, and now publishes a quarterly art magazine. He's a mentor to other career searchers and is living an authentic life.

Did his setback stunt his growth and progress? Not in the least. In fact, he turned the failure into motivation and continued to make more and more internally-aligned decisions. You can do that too.

**Go All In**

We talked about not getting stuck at the trailhead and not letting obstacles stop you. But what I really hope for you is that you'll take on that trail with zeal. Get after it! I want you to go all in. I mean, you've done all this work to learn about who you are as a person and what makes you unique. You've done the research to connect who you are with real-world careers. Another way to think about that is that you've found a connection between what you do well, what you are likely to derive satisfaction from, and a genuine need in the world.

Stop for a second and think about how compelling that is.

You are in a position to add value to a field of work that you truly care about. As in, you could use your unique talents to make the world a better place.

So what can you do to maximize your experiences as you move forward along your career path?

Declaring your major and registering for classes are the next logical step. A department advisor can be a good resource at this time if they can give you information about available classes, tracks and extracurriculars associated with your academic department. They may be able to give you insights about how other students have made the most of their academic experience. They may also have information about volunteer opportunities and internships that are available.

Remember, you're still in the process of discovering your best-fit career. As we talked about in the first chapter, major is just a part of the picture. In order to be really informed about how your career will look, it's important to seek out meaningful experiences outside the classroom. You should take advantage of any opportunity that helps you gain clarity about what life could look like in that major, field, or career including internship opportunities, summer jobs, fellowships, continuing to connect with professionals, reading books relevant to the topic, volunteering with an organization that does this work, and more. In addition to increasing your understanding of the field, these experiences outside of the classroom can help you develop a stronger sense for the facets of the field that you feel most strongly about and a better understanding of where you are best equipped to add value.

You've got to find the balance between expanding your vision through conversations, research, experiences and reflection while also simply taking steps forward. One of my favorite anecdotes comes from Boyd K. Packer, a lifelong educator and ecclesiastical leader. He was struggling with a challenging problem and saw no way forward. He approached a mentor, Harold B. Lee, for advice, who said this:

"The trouble with you is you want to see the end from the beginning.' I replied that I would like to see at least a step or two ahead. Then came the lesson of a lifetime: 'You must learn to walk to the edge of the light, and then a few steps into the darkness; then the light will appear and show the way before you." (President Boyd K. Packer, President of the Quorum of the Twelve Apostles, "The Edge of the Light," BYU Magazine, Mar. 1991, magazine.byu.edu.)

# Chapter 13

## A Few Final Encouragements

You've made it. If you've followed along, you are clearer than you've ever been about who you are at your best. You have explored several majors and begun to circle around a few. You've connected with your constellation of contacts and are starting to feel some momentum. And you've made a decision, or at least decided to decide soon. Don't let the deadline force the decision. Just be intentional and proactive. Act, rather than being acted upon.

I'll close by sharing a few thoughts in the last chapter from the thousands of career searchers I've worked with over the past 20 years, from the 14-year-old ambitious planner to the 72-year-old reinventing their path. But I'll preview that advice by saying this: the same principles that apply at 14 and at 21 as a college student apply at 72 as a career resetter:

Step One: Reflect

Step Two: Explore

Step Three: Connect

Then decide.

The process is simple. And yet it isn't. It asks you to invest significant time and effort. Although you've gotten a lot of clarity on your choice of college major, you've got a whole lifetime of career decisions ahead of you and it is possible that you will find yourself feeling overwhelmed again. If you find yourself feeling overwhelmed, consider the following.

**Incrementalization**

How do you eat an elephant?

Incrementally. One bite at a time...or so I hear.

Incrementalization.

I'm not even sure that's a word based on the red squiggly line I'm getting from Microsoft Word, but the concept is definitely true.

Incrementalization is all about small steps done consistently over time to lead to an ultimate outcome.

To give credit where it's due, my good friend Aaron coined the term. He trained for an ultra-marathon awhile back, one of those crazy 50-mile races that no one does unless they're insane. He was talking about training and said it's all about breaking it down. If you think of it as a 50-mile run, you'll get overwhelmed. But if you think about it as ten five-mile runs it becomes doable.

All great things come incrementally. Ultra-marathons. Investing. Dieting. Education. Exercise. Spirituality.

And...wait for it...

Career. Or more specifically, loving what you do and getting paid to do it.

The goal in choosing a major and career path is incrementalization — taking small steps that get you closer to your best-fit career. The challenge comes when you try to take the leap from a job you hate straight to a job you love, or from having no idea what to do for a career to locking yourself into something for the long haul, believing that what appeals to you at 21 will still be a fit at 52.

That's tough and can be discouraging.

When I decided I didn't like what I was doing, I took a step. And another. And another. And with each step, I analyzed what I liked and didn't like and used that self-reflection to guide the next step.

This past week I met with someone who belongs in the State Department, another person who'd make a great counselor, a future politician, and an entrepreneur in the making. None of these people are actually in these careers, or really anything close to them. But that's okay, because the goal isn't to get there now; the goal is simply to make sure their next step gets them closer.

Where they end up may not be in these areas at all but heading toward them means they have a stronger likelihood of landing in something congruent with who they are.

If you're feeling stuck, try reducing the size of the bite you're trying to take. You can't eat an elephant all at once. You also can't land a dream job in one leap. The good news is, you don't have to. Just take one step in the direction you want to go.

Try one bite at a time.

### Career is not linear

You will almost never end where you started.

At 15, I wanted to be the President. By 22, I was majoring in public relations. On my 30th birthday, I was teaching leadership classes at

Rice University. And at 43, I'm running a leadership development consultancy. What's the common thread?

Who knows. Perhaps all of these careers are connected by a desire to influence humankind. Or maybe the throughline is leadership, and my desire to learn how to be a better leader. Hindsight has a way of making sense of things that were perhaps nonsensical. In the rearview mirror it all seems to connect, but in the moment it sure felt random and disconnected. And that's okay.

One thing that's clear is I never guessed that I'd be where I am today doing what I'm doing. And the same is true for you.

As much as we want for our careers to be a logical series of steps that result in an ultimate outcome, they almost never are. In reality, at each step or in every job you'll revisit the principles discussed in this book and reflect, explore, and connect.

To be fair, we're socialized into this thinking from a young age. You work your way through 12 grades to go to college, where you'll work your way through four years to get a job. You'll work your way through team member, manager, and director, to ultimately be a vice president. Or from medical student to resident to fellow, to one day be a physician.

We're hard-wired for preplanned paths.

And yet, career looks more like a squiggly line on a treasure map with ups and downs and detours. And there really is no "X" marking "the spot," because there is no spot! The goal of career is to choose authenticity, and success looks like every job getting you closer and closer to being your authentic self every day and getting paid to do it.

Is vision important? Certainly. If you don't know where you're going, it's difficult to know what path to take to get there. But it's also important to make the decision right in front of you, do the best you can, be reflective, and then take the next step.

Career doesn't operate on a straight line.

## It's Called Work for a Reason

All right. So, I've got to address this one last thing because if I hear it one more time, I'll lose my mind.

"But Dustin, is it really realistic to love what you do all the time? I mean, aren't there parts of all jobs that you're going to dislike?"

*Yes.* There are parts of all jobs you are going to dislike.

But I'll tell you this — if I'm creating a strategic plan because I've been told to by my boss, I've got a different level of energy than if I'm developing a strategic plan for my business, Proof Leadership Group. I don't love the task either way, but with the second example, I love it as part of a bigger, more meaningful work.

Another example: I just spent three hours drafting invoices, agreements, and proposals for my company. Did I love it? No. Do I love owning my own company, despite those painful tasks?

Emphatically *yes.*

Can you love your work, but still have to do lame stuff? Yes. But if the lame stuff outweighs the great stuff something's wrong. That's what I'm trying to address. I live and work for those of you who, when I ask what portion of your week you love, answer less than 50%.

I'm not here to absolve you from having to do hard things and tasks that aren't meaningful.

I'm here to help you find meaningful work the majority of the time so that those painful tasks wreak less havoc and become part of a bigger, more empowering and awesome picture.

So, what is the gold standard you should aim for? As I mentioned in chapter 6, I often tell my clients the goal is a 70% fit. Think of that for a moment. What would it feel like if 70% of the time each week you did something you love to do? Something that aligns with who you are? You were simply getting paid to be you? That would be 28 hours of a 40-hour work week spent in your passion. And getting paid. That's incredible! That would mean two to three hours a day doing stuff you don't like for the opportunity to spend five to six hours a day in your bliss. Wow. I'll take that any day. Especially because what you'll find is that you'll craft your career over time to make it more and more of who you are. You may start at 70%, but you'll end at 90%. You will have made it, my friend.

**Go All In**

So, get started! Here's a final reminder of the process:

1. Get radically clear about who you are at your best.
2. Explore options, beginning to surface opportunities. Be divergent, not convergent!
3. Connect with people. The gap between ambiguity and clarity is filled by people who have been there and done

that. Also, it turns out people are the ones who will offer you internships and jobs. They are pretty important to get to know.

4.  Decide! But not until you've done Steps 1-3. If you've done your due diligence and listened to your inner voice, just pick something and go with it. It's not final. You're not choosing one path forever. My own path has bobbed and weaved and that's just how it works. I started in Public Relations, tried Sales, leaped to Student Affairs, taught Leadership at two universities, joined the K-12 Charter school movement, launched Proof Leadership Group, wrote three books, dabbled in career coaching, invested in real estate, and maybe one day I'll tame lions. Career is a journey, not an event. You can always change as you learn more about the field and yourself.

And remember: there is no one right, so you can't choose wrong.

As you've worked through this book, you've learned so much about who you are and how you can contribute to the world. That in itself is huge. Trust that your inner voice will speak up if you head down a path that isn't aligned.

Remember, inspiration comes when you take action, so act. Pick a path and start walking it. You can only research and explore for so long before it's time to take a step into the unknown. If you've done the work, you're ready. Trust yourself and enjoy the journey. You are well on your way to a major and career you love.

Find your fit and choose it.

# About the Author

Dustin Peterson has led high-impact leadership training and career coaching for more than fifteen years. He is the founder and President at Proof Leadership Group, a leadership consultancy focused on building outstanding cultures where people thrive. As a trainer, coach, and consultant in the private, public, and nonprofit sectors, he has helped more than 200 companies and thousands of individuals do more of what they do best.

Dustin completed his MS in educational leadership from Indiana University and his BS in communications at Brigham Young University–Idaho.

He is the author of *Reset: How to Get Paid and Love What You Do* and *Talented: Discovering and Using Your God-Given Talents to Find More Joy in Life* and lives in Houston with his wife and four kids.

You can connect with Dustin at dustin@proofleadership.com, via Instagram @dustinpeterson, or by visiting his site at www.dustinpeterson.org or www.proofleadership.com.

# Notes

# Notes

# Notes

# Notes

# Notes

# Notes

# Notes

# Notes

# Notes

# Notes

www.ingramcontent.com/pod-product-compliance
Lightning Source LLC
Chambersburg PA
CBHW060835220526
45466CB00003B/1109